Fighting the Demon of Suicide

by

Coach Doug Merrill

Copyright © 2008

ISBN: 978-0-9802184-0-4

All rights reserved. No part of this book may be reproduced or transmitted in any form or by any means, electronic or mechanical, including photocopying, recording, or by information storage and retrieval systems, without the written permission of the publisher, except by a reviewer who may quote brief passages in a review.

Printed in the United States of America

Contents

Dedication.............................	v
Foreword.............................	vii
Preface.............................	xi
Chapter 1. Kevin.......................	1
Chapter 2. Dawn.......................	11
Chapter 3. Samantha....................	32
Chapter 4. An Accident.................	48
Chapter 5. A Meeting by Chance..........	57
Chapter 6. What If?....................	64
Chapter 7. Tyler's Fight.................	73
Chapter 8. Derek.......................	80
Chapter 9. The Morning Call.............	107
Chapter 10. My Morning Off.............	113
Chapter 11. More Alarms................	136
Chapter 12. A Message from Coach Merrill...	147
Web Resources.........................	159

Dedication

To the Bowling Green High School classes of 1989, 2006, and 2007. You truly were and continue to be my inspiration. Your energy and encouragement give me the strength to continue the fight against the silence of suicide.

In addition, I would like to recognize and thank all of the families that are mentioned in this book. I commend you for your courage and thank you for your support. Also, to my brave editor, Joyce, thank you for all of your hours of hard work. You brought out the best in my writing, proving how talented you truly are as mentor, teacher, and friend.

Further, I thank my family for all that they are and continue to be. I will always be proud of you and love you, no matter what life obstacles come our way.

Lastly, I dedicate this book to all of you: students, teachers, administrators, coaches, and parents. I hope my experiences with suicide and depression will help you understand more about mental illness, and I pray my message of hope, faith, and love will leave you feeling empowered and motivated to do more with your life. Together, we can all learn to be more tolerant and compassionate people.

Foreword

Suicide is a significant public health problem. The statistics connected to suicide completions and attempts are alarming, both in terms of the sheer numbers that they reflect but also because of the human suffering they represent. In 2004, there were roughly 33,000 suicides, or 90 suicides each day in the United States. Suicide ranks as the THIRD leading cause of death for young people ages 15–24 and FOURTH for ages 10–14. Shockingly, suicide is the SECOND leading cause of death for our college-age adults, as well as for youth ages 15 to 19 in many states. In 2000, although no official government records were maintained, it is estimated that over one million youth attempted suicide in the U.S. That equates to over 2,700 attempts each day in our nation by adolescent youth ages 12 to 17. As if these statistics concerning attempts were not worrisome enough, the death toll for completed suicides is staggering. Each week in our nation, we have approximately 100+ young people die by suicide. In the past 40 years, youth suicide death rates have almost tripled. Between 1980 and 1996, suicide rates for the youngest ages for which statistics were recorded (ages 10 to 14) increased by over 100 percent. The frightening truth is that more teenagers and young adults have died of suicide than from cancer, heart disease, AIDS, birth defects, stroke, pneumonia, influenza, and chronic lung disease COMBINED. Suicide is truly a silent epidemic that is claiming the lives of children, adolescents, and young adults.

After reading the statistics above, you may be asking yourself: "What is behind this silent epidemic?" and "Is there anything that can be done to solve this serious problem?"

In my opinion, there are two main reasons why the problem of suicide infects our society at the level of a national public health crisis. The first reason is that of STIGMA. Stigma, as it relates to suicide specifically, is the bias held by the general public against those who suffer from mental and emotional disorders. Our historical misunderstanding, segregation, and maltreatment of those with mental illness still haunt us today. Most of us would rather cope with almost any "physical" disease than admit that our child may be suffering with major depression, bipolar disorder, a substance abuse disorder, or an anxiety disorder. Yet we know that 90 percent of completed suicides result from undiagnosed or untreated mental illnesses. Our biases against recognizing and treating mental illness lead to the fact that many suicides are not reported as such but rather as accidental deaths. As staggering as the statistics above may seem, they are grossly underreported, with some experts asserting by as much as 30 percent!

The second major reason is quite simply our public mental health care system is not adequately funded to provide for the capacity of need or for easy access of care required by our society. Access in a timely manner to quality mental health care is a significant issue that directly relates to the number of suicides we have in our communities. Many times there are not adequately trained clinicians who have had specific training in suicide assessment, and there are definitely far too few psychiatrists who specialize in the care of children. Frankly, the conditions concerning stigma and treatment access for suicidal individuals are truly awful. Even though four out of five people who attempt suicide communicate with another person their intent prior to their attempt, only about one-third of them ever get any mental health treatment.

What about our second question: "Is there anything that can be done to solve this serious problem?" The answer is a resounding YES. The majority of suicides are preventable if we are willing to take an interest in protecting others' welfare by becoming a gatekeeper. "Gatekeepers" are not clinicians, and they do not diagnose mental illness; rather as a gatekeeper, we learn to recognize the signs and symptoms of mental illnesses that underlie suicidality and are willing to step forward to help another individual in need to access professional care. As a gatekeeper, we are willing to set aside our fears of getting involved and we are willing to ask someone if they need help or tell someone who can assist the person in getting help.

In addition to our individual willingness to serve as gatekeepers, we also need to come together as a concerned group of citizens. A public grass roots effort is now underway with its major message being to no longer tolerate the rates of death and suffering among our young people. A public outcry to our political leaders to fund and support suicide prevention programs is desperately needed. Fortunately, local communities in Ohio are organizing "Suicide Prevention Coalitions," many of which are funded by a new statewide suicide prevention foundation: The Ohio Suicide Prevention Foundation. These coalitions are made up of concerned individuals from many diverse segments of the community. Suicide Coalitions can provide assistance in organizing events and increasing awareness in their local communities, helping to reduce stigma, and they also can provide a voice to state and national leaders on the importance of tackling suicide as a significant public health problem.

Doug Merrill is not alone in his connection to suicide. In Ohio, we have over 1,200 suicides each year. It is estimated that for each completed suicide, there are over six people (family and friends), or "suicide survivors," left behind. That means each year in Ohio alone, we have some 7,200 suicide survivors who are coping with the loss of a loved one to suicide. I have never given training or a speech on the topic of suicide in our region, nationally, or internationally without someone in the audience coming up to me after the talk and sharing with me their loss related to suicide.

Doug is passionate about his work in helping to educate others about suicide and its terrible aftermath because he knows firsthand how devastating the suicide deaths are for family and friends. He has dedicated himself to helping prevent suicides through raising awareness, lowering stigma, and by fund-raising. Doug believes in providing positive alternatives for children and adolescents who may be discouraged or suffering with a mental or emotional disorder. I fully support Doug in his efforts to reach out and make a difference in our communities.

Paul F. Granello, Ph.D., LPCC
Associate Professor, The Ohio State University &
Chief Science Officer, The Ohio Suicide Prevention Foundation

Preface

It was not my intent to write a book on suicide or depression. I only intended to write down some of my thoughts and feelings concerning the past couple of days and what seemed like a lifetime of dealing with death, suicide, and depression.

Over the course of my life, I have coped with the losses of eight suicides and the suicide attempt of three. After writing what amounts to being the first two chapters of the book, I shared my work with our high school's librarian. She gave me the encouragement to continue writing about my past and my feelings about teenage depression and suicide.

I took her advice and continued writing; however, I did not want to simply give the accounts of my experiences with suicide. I also wanted to leave my readers with an understanding of depression and to give them a plan for beating their demon of suicide.

In our society, we often fear issues that we do not understand. Suicide is certainly one of those issues. Even in my hometown where we have had several suicides in recent years, some people are still uncomfortable talking about it. It amazes me. Many feel that talking about suicide will only cause more suicides.

I find that attitude incomprehensible, because not talking about it did not prevent the suicides that we did have. I believe opening the lines of communication with our children, students, players, and community is the only way to break through the walls of stigma and ignorance that time has put up.

This has been the biggest reason for writing the book. I want to destroy the stigma of mental illness. Stigma is killing our society. Depression is real, and it is a disease—a medical condition. It should be treated no differently than cancer or any other lethal medical diagnoses, and if gone untreated, it will have the same results.

In addition, I hope to bring even more attention to the national fight for mental health parity between physical and mental health rights for those who suffer from mental illness. I believe even more can be done for those who do not have the economic means to continue their treatment. Imagine if someone told you that you can only have three chemotherapy treatments opposed to the 12 that you would need to treat your cancer.

I hope that all of you who read this book and may be suffering from depression understand that *it is OK* to seek and accept help. Do not be a fool; if you would accept a cast for a broken leg, then you should accept help and treat your depression.

As a baseball coach for nearly 20 years, I have given many speeches about winning, losing, building character, and overcoming adversity. I have told my teams for years that character does not define you by the events that happen in your life. Your character is defined by how you *deal* with those events.

I would not trade any of my adversities, bumps in the road, or pain that I have had to endure for anything. All of those things are what make me who I am and what have given me the strength to teach and help others overcome their adversities and to encourage others to do their very best.

Chapter 1

Kevin

It was May of 1987. I was a sophomore at Bowling Green High School, and other than the typical problems that all high school kids go through, all was normal. I can remember when all of that changed. I was sitting in the family room at my parents' home when the phone rang.

"Hello," I said, answering the phone.
"Doug, it's John. I have something to tell you."
"What's up, John?" I asked.
"It's Kevin. He's dead."

I could hardly believe the words that I had just heard. *Kevin was dead?* Kevin and I had been friends since we met in the first grade. We shared the same teachers through elementary school and during our junior high years. In addition, we were on the school's wrestling team together. When I received the call informing me of Kevin's death, we were only 16, and 16 year olds aren't supposed to die.

"*What?* Is this some sort of joke?" I asked John, thinking that it wasn't very funny if it were.

"I'm afraid not, Doug. He's dead."

"How? How did he die?" I asked.

The answer only brought more surprise and shock.

"He committed suicide. He killed himself," my friend said.

"I know what suicide is, John," I answered.

I was baffled. Apparently, Kevin felt that his problems were different from mine or anyone else's. Kevin must have felt that he could not seek help for his problems and that all hope had been lost. As a result, he went into his parents' garage and decided to leave this world with a rope around his neck.

Kevin's suicide didn't make any sense to me. I had just seen Kevin the day before, and he made no mention of anything that was bothering him. There were no signs, no warnings, and no conversations that could have given us a clue about his impending demise. He wasn't crying about anything, and he wasn't at odds with anyone that I knew of. None of it made sense.

I remember feeling that someone was playing a trick on me. I wanted to go over to Kevin's house to see him, to foil the joke, but the telephone rang over and over again. I spent most of my day on the phone with several of my friends, talking about the same thing. Kevin had died by suicide.

The drama of Kevin's death unfolded over the next few days. I can remember going to school after Kevin committed suicide, still hoping that I would see him and hoping that his suicide was nothing more than a cruel joke. It wasn't long, however, until the reality of Kevin's death set in. I noticed that the flag in front of the school was at half-mast, and in the hallways, I could see students in front of their lockers, crying and expressing their grief. There were also grief counselors in the hallways and in the offices doing what they could to counsel students.

I remember having no interest in talking with any of the counselors, instead, preferring only to exchange thoughts about Kevin's suicide with my friends. We discussed how he did it, when he did it, who found him, who, if anyone, was home at the time, how long it might have taken him to die, whether he had struggled to get out of the noose in an attempt to change his mind, etc. But most of all we asked, *why?* That was the one question none of us could answer.

Reality of Kevin's death continued to hit all of us in the face as his funeral arrangements were made known. There was to be a night of visitation at the funeral home, followed by the funeral at the junior high auditorium the next day. I wanted to go and pay my last respects to Kevin and to talk with his family, but I was a little nervous. I had been to funerals before, but never to a funeral of someone my own age.

It was not the first time I had heard the word "suicide" or known someone who had ended his own life. When I was only 11 years old, Harry, a neighbor who lived across the street from me, committed suicide in his garage. It happened on a Friday afternoon, and, due to a teacher workday, we had the day off from school. It was a sunny day, and my friends and I had been playing whiffle ball since early that morning. At approximately 3:00 p.m., Harry's wife, Shelby, and her 4-year-old daughter pulled into the driveway and opened the garage door. All of us who were playing whiffle ball suddenly stopped playing at the sound of Shelby's screams. We looked across the street to see what had caused her panic. We caught a glimpse of Harry lying on the floor of the garage by the car with his head next to the back tire. At first, I wasn't sure how serious the situation was. I figured that he had fallen and knocked himself out or something like that.

Everything seemed to move very quickly from that point. It was like watching a movie in fast-forward motion.

Another neighbor who lived next to Harry and Shelby came running out of his garage and began to assist Shelby. He called 911 and whisked their daughter inside the house next door. Within minutes, the ambulance came roaring around the corner of the street with the lights and sirens blaring. Seconds after arriving, paramedics began CPR in an attempt to save Harry's life. All the while, my friends and I stood in the front yard witnessing the events unfolding before us. For several minutes, paramedics continued to work feverishly to try to revive Harry. The severity of the situation hit me when I saw the paramedics wheeling Harry's lifeless body from the garage to the back of the ambulance. Harry's arm had fallen from his side and was dragging on the driveway. The paramedics noticed and secured the arm to Harry's side. The second sign that indicated the gravity of Harry's condition came as I watched the ambulance leave without speeding or blaring its sirens, as it had done upon arrival.

Later that evening, word had spread through the neighborhood that Harry had committed suicide by carbon monoxide poisoning. Harry was only in his 30s and had left behind a wife and child. With Harry's death, I was exposed to suicide for the first time in my life.

Now, 5 years later, a friend of mine had chosen the same fate as Harry. I snapped back to the reality of the emotional scene at the funeral home—Kevin's visitation. Kevin was not some neighbor I knew from a distance, but rather my friend. There were students, teachers, parents, family members, and friends all there to pay their respects to Kevin and to show their support to his immediate family. None of us really knew what to say to them. What could we say? None of us could make sense of what had happened, and we could only imagine what they were going through. Most of us just stared at each other and wondered the same thing: How did this happen to our friend? Why did he not tell us of his struggles and problems that overwhelmed him, and how could we not see his pain?

The day of Kevin's funeral was not any easier. My friends and I drove to the junior high for the funeral. We were first met by some of our old teachers and the principal from the junior high. It was strange. We spoke briefly about things that had nothing to do with Kevin's death. We discussed how we liked the high school, how our classes were going, and how the wrestling season had gone. We all knew why we had come together again at the junior high, but none of us spoke of Kevin or his suicide.

As we entered the auditorium, I was remembering the many times I'd been there in the past with my classmates for drama productions, concerts, and assemblies. Those were happier times, and most of those memories included Kevin.

My friends and I sat down at the end of an aisle, about halfway to the center stage. We looked at what I remember as a memorial card that briefly outlined Kevin's life. As we sat waiting for the ceremony to begin, we continued to talk about anything except the real reason we were there—Kevin's funeral. I think emotional exhaustion was beginning to set in, and I guess it was easier for us to talk about other things.

All of that changed, however, when Kevin's parents, sister, and the rest of his family walked in. The auditorium became silent. At that point, the only thing anyone heard was the occasional whimper of sadness that filled the auditorium. Everyone in the room sat in silence. We all just stared at Kevin's family as they came in. It did not take long before I felt a lump in the middle of my throat.

I was fighting it. I didn't want to cry again, and I didn't want to be the first of my friends to cry either. However, it did not get any easier. As Kevin's coffin was wheeled from the back of the auditorium to the front, I felt the lump in my throat grow larger and my eyes start to fill with tears.

The combination of seeing Kevin's family in so much pain, watching everyone in the room break down at the scene playing itself out, and realizing that I would never see my friend again was too much to bear. I was feeling the sword of sadness that was cutting through the auditorium.

"Bridge over Troubled Water" was the song being played as we waited for the reverend to begin the service. I will never forget that music. I had never before heard such a sad song, or maybe it just had new meaning for me. Whatever it was, I remember how powerful and painful it was to hear. It made me sad and gave me clarity. It was clear that we were not there for a pep assembly or a play or a concert. We were there because our friend had committed suicide.

"We didn't have to be here. Kevin didn't have to kill himself," I thought.

A new emotion now was starting to set in—anger!

I was becoming angry because I was sad. I was angry for what Kevin had done to his parents, sister, family, friends, teachers, and all who had never dealt with death or suicide and were now forced to do so. I began to wonder. How could Kevin, who had always put everyone else first, commit such a selfish act and think of no one but himself?

I also wondered whether Kevin had considered or anticipated the impact his death was going to have on all of us. Did he know his suicide would hurt us so much? And if he did, why didn't he reverse his decision? These are two questions I will never be able to answer. The fact remained that we were there, grieving with unanswered questions and listening to a song that would forever be linked, in my mind, to Kevin and to suicide.

As the service progressed with speeches and music, I found myself daydreaming. I began to remember the times that Kevin and I had spent together. My fondest memory of Kevin was at a wrestling tournament when we were in junior high.

The tournament was beginning to wind down. It had been a long day, and I wasn't exactly feeling very good about myself at the time because I had finished fourth. Kevin, who had also finished for the day, had ranked first. I was sulking in the cafeteria by myself when Kevin approached. I remember him patting me on the back and telling me, "You'll get 'em next time." I was not as confident as Kevin, but when I looked up at him, he smiled, and that made me feel better. Kevin then stood up and said, "Let's get something to eat."

"I'm out of money," I answered.

I was somewhat embarrassed and still a little blue from the results of the wrestling tournament.

"I've got you," Kevin replied with his arm around my shoulders and helping me to my feet.

With those thoughts on my mind, I began to smile and shake my head a little.

"That was Kevin," I thought.

Kevin always thought of everyone else before he thought of himself. He was one of those "popular" kids. Everyone liked him. I don't remember anyone who didn't like him. Kevin had that way about him, as only a few have. He had that ability to light up a room any time he walked into it. Even those who didn't know him personally knew who he was.

As I sat in the auditorium smiling at those memories, reality hit me again. Kevin's sister had taken the podium and began to talk about her brother. The sadness in her voice summed up what everyone in the room was feeling: hopelessness, emptiness, and fear. We felt all of those emotions because we were not ever to see

Kevin again. The lump in my throat only grew larger as I sat and listened to her voice. I would have done anything to take the pain from her, from all of us.

After the service, my friends and I walked outside to the sidewalk across from the parking lot. It was a madhouse! It seemed as if the entire group of students, teachers, administrators, family, and friends had congregated outside. I remember people in cars passing by and staring at all of us. I felt I could almost read their minds: "That's the funeral for that kid that killed himself."

The whole day seemed like one big orchestrated production. It began to feel like theater, and we were all actors in a play.

The scene on the sidewalk was no different from the scene we had just left inside the auditorium. Many of us were hugging and crying as we tried to make sense of our loss. I, too, was standing on the sidewalk with some of my friends. We were gathering and deciding who was going to ride with whom out to the cemetery. As I began to get into the car, I looked down the street and saw Dawn.

Dawn had been a girlfriend of mine, and it appeared that she was having trouble with the funeral scene. I don't know why I singled her out because everyone seemed to be struggling with the loss of Kevin, but she seemed to be handling it differently from everyone else. I thought of walking over to speak with her, but she was surrounded by her girlfriends, so I continued into the car thinking that I would see her either at the cemetery or later in the day.

The cemetery scene was perhaps the toughest of the day. It was fast and to the point. We walked from the car to the tent were Kevin's body was to be laid for the final time. The coffin, which held Kevin's body, sat patiently in the hearse as his mourners gathered. The coffin was then marched under the tent and placed on the brass bars that were in front of Kevin's family, who were seated in front of the waiting grave.

The reverend began by gathering people in closer and starting with a prayer. He spoke from scripture, then went on to recite another prayer, and then it was over. I remember how fast the service was. Just like that, we were being asked to return to our cars. We were to leave and never to be with Kevin again. One by one, those who came returned to their cars and drove away. It was over!

I hadn't realized it at the time but part of what comforted me about going to the funeral home and to the funeral itself was the knowledge that I was going to be with Kevin again, or at least his body, during those events and everything was still going to be okay. As long as those events were in our lives, Kevin was still in our lives. Now at the cemetery, it was setting in. I was not going to be with him anymore. Now I would only have my memories. There weren't going to be any more services for our friend. There wasn't going to be a tomorrow for Kevin. No more wrestling tournaments, no more pizza parties, no sleepovers. Kevin would never again have the chance to enjoy video games or play football in the backyard. He would never again hang out with his friends or go to school dances. Kevin would never marry or have a family, and Kevin would never again be able to hug his mom or learn from his dad.

Family functions for Kevin's family would forever be changed as well. All holidays would be hollow and incomplete. We were leaving Kevin at the cemetery, and we were to go on without him. I was now feeling cold and sad, not only for Kevin, but also for his family and myself.

Later that day, several of us gathered at various friends' houses. We shared stories of Kevin and laughed and cried, but we also knew that tomorrow would come and Kevin would no longer be with us. It would be difficult to imagine life without him. He was a good friend and teammate.

For me, the following days were difficult and were filled with thoughts of my own mortality. I began to realize how fragile life truly is. I had several conversations with my parents about life and death. I remember telling my parents how difficult it was to go to school, to go to places where Kevin and I had been, and to laugh or think about having a good time again. My mom and dad understood my feelings and tried to reassure me that each day would be better. I can remember hoping they were right. I wanted to move forward and live life, but I wanted to do so without feeling guilty or feeling that I was betraying my friend.

Losing a friend is hard enough for anyone to go through, but for a young person, it especially brings confusion. Kids are left wondering about their own mortality and what happens when people die. It's a thought process and conversation that we all go through at some point, and it raises even more questions when the death is by suicide. It becomes difficult to move forward and live our own lives.

Unfortunately, none of us would get the chance to let time heal any of our wounds or sorrows. Tragedy would soon strike us once again.

Chapter 2

Dawn

The days after Kevin's funeral were met with the challenge of moving forward. Several of us still had questions about death, and we particularly struggled over the issue of suicide. Among my schoolmates, including my good friend and former girlfriend Dawn, there were two nagging questions: Why couldn't we see Kevin's suicide coming, and did Kevin go to heaven or hell?

Dawn and I had been friends for approximately 3½ years. I will never forget the first time I saw her. It was the first day of school in seventh-grade math class, and our teacher, Mr. Smith, was explaining the syllabus and telling us what would be expected from us. I sat in the back row next to the door, and Dawn sat in the third row and in the middle of the room. I was unable to take my eyes off of her. I fell in love with Dawn the way only a seventh-grader can, and in the weeks ahead, we began "going together." Dawn and I went together for the next 2 years.

We had ended the relationship of boyfriend and girlfriend for reasons that I can't even remember. I'm sure it was for some reason that we would consider dumb or juvenile today, but I'm sure the reasons seemed real and important then. Things always do at that age. Luckily, for me, Dawn and I remained good friends, genuinely close friends. In some regards, we were better friends after we broke up than when we were dating.

Dawn and I were in the choir together, as well as in several English and math classes, and we talked on the phone until either her parents or my parents would yell at us to hang up. We even went to school dances with each other when we didn't have other dates, which was most of the time. I guess we still had a soft spot for one another.

When Kevin committed suicide, Dawn and I were in the tenth grade and at the time, neither of us was old enough to drive. Instead, we rode the same bus home and sat in the same seats every day for the ride home. I sat in the third to last seat on the left, and Dawn rode in the second to last seat of the same side. Every day our bus traveled from the high school to the junior high where some students were dropped off and others were picked up. From the junior high, the bus took us home to the neighborhood where we both lived. It was as routine as the sun coming up in the morning.

On Wednesday after Kevin died, the school was still reeling over the suicide. On the bus that day after school, I went down the aisle to my usual seat, but I noticed that Dawn was staring out of the window. I remember making a comment to her—probably something "smart" in my daily attempt to evoke a laugh from her. It didn't take me long, though, to realize that something was wrong. She was quiet and certainly not in the mood for my jokes. I quickly changed my demeanor and asked,

"What's wrong, Dawn?"

Dawn looked back out the window and paused, but only for a moment. She then turned her head and attention back toward me and began to explain to me that many of her friends and fellow classmates had said that Kevin had gone to hell for committing suicide. Dawn went on to explain how some of her friends mentioned that it is written in the Bible that those who commit suicide are condemned to hell for eternity.

The idea of Kevin, or anyone else for that matter, going to hell for committing suicide bothered Dawn a great deal. I can still visualize her—so sad, so confused, so tormented—sitting in the corner of her seat. I didn't have to be a psychologist to see that she was struggling with the idea that Kevin might still be in pain. I had never seen Dawn like that before. Our conversation that day would be one I would never forget and one that would haunt me for the rest of my life. Until now, I have shared the conversation with only a few people.

"Do you think Kevin went to hell for killing himself?" Dawn asked.

"No, I don't think he's in hell. Who told you that?"

I recall her sad and confused face and remember wanting to do whatever it took to make her feel better.

"Just kids in school. They said that when people kill themselves, they go to hell."

"I don't believe that, Dawn," I stated.

"What do you believe happened to Kevin?" she asked with great curiosity.

"Dawn, I believe that when it's our time to die, we will be able to see and talk to Kevin the same as we are talking to each other now."

I spoke with great urgency, realizing that Dawn was seriously troubled; at the same time, I was encouraged to feel that my comments seemed to bring her some comfort.

As our bus left the parking lot of the high school, we continued our talk about the afterlife and suicide. During our conversation, Dawn at one point said she was supposed to get off the bus at the junior high. From there she would walk to the courthouse to meet her mother, who was working there on a case. However, Dawn did not get off the bus as planned. Instead, we continued our conversation on the bus, which had already begun its journey to our neighborhood.

Why Dawn didn't get off at the junior high as planned, I don't remember. I know she must have given me a reason that I was satisfied with. In any case, she did not get off, and we continued our journey home.

Through our conversation, I was feeling good about myself for helping Dawn feel better. She seemed to be more at peace. On the rest of the trip home, we continued to discuss Kevin, life and death, suicide, and heaven vs. hell. As we neared our stop, Dawn asked me if I would come in to the house so we could continue our talk or do something about it.

After talking for approximately another 20 minutes or so, I reminded Dawn that it was the opening day of the town mall where my aunt was opening a store. My mother was expecting me home so we could go see the new shopping mall. I told her that I couldn't come in, but I would see her tonight at choir practice and we could continue our discussion then. Dawn nodded her head, entered her home, and closed the front door behind her.

I continued to walk down the street to my house. The whole time, I was congratulating myself about doing a great job to make her feel better. I even recall telling my mother about how I made Dawn feel better. I did not go into any details, only to say that Dawn had been upset about Kevin's death and that I tried to help her feel better.

After returning home from the mall, I began my chores, which included cutting the grass. I was wearing my headphones and listening to music as I made my laps back and forth when I heard sirens. I removed the headphones only for a moment to hear the sounds, which seemed to be coming closer. I remember thinking to myself, "I hope it's not Dawn." I shrugged the idea off. I suppose I thought of Dawn because of the conversation we had had on the way home from school earlier in the day.

As I was putting the mower in the garage, my dad poked his head out and told me that I had a phone call. I went inside and picked up the phone. In the next few seconds, everything that I thought I was sure of in life was suddenly gone.

The voice on the other end of the line was my friend Zach, who lived next door. He was also one of the students that we picked up from the junior high before we continued home on the bus.

"Hey, Zach, what's up?" I asked.

"Doug, did you hear about Dawn? She tried to kill herself."

I was a little surprised at my reaction, but I didn't burst into tears or fall on the floor wailing. I simply and calmly asked him if she had succeeded. I must have asked Zach that question at least three times. Each time, Zach replied the same, "I don't know." All he knew was that she had tried to commit suicide by hanging herself with a rope in her basement. Dawn had tried to end her life the same way that Kevin had, by her own hands and by hanging.

My dad was in the kitchen where I had taken the call. He knew by the sound of my voice on the phone that something was wrong. After hanging up the phone, I put both of my hands over my face and began to cry.

"No, no, no," I said repeatedly.

My dad came to my side and put his arms around me, asking over and over again what was wrong. I finally told him that Dawn had tried to kill herself. He didn't know what to say. He kept telling me over and over again how sorry he was. Looking back now, I can remember the look he had on his face. It was fear. He thought of Kevin and now was thinking that Dawn's death may have been a copycat suicide.

Within minutes, the doorbell rang. The front door was open, leaving only the glass storm door to see through. It was Zach. He had come over to see how I was doing.

I stepped outside on the porch to talk. I was in a state of disbelief. It was the same feeling that I had when I heard of Kevin's suicide. I wanted to believe that it was all some sort of a joke. We decided to walk down toward Dawn's house to see if anything was going on. I opened the storm door and yelled into the house that Zach and I were going for a walk and would be right back. My dad looked apprehensive but nodded his approval. I let go of the door, and we started down the street.

We were hardly halfway down the street when a police car passed us heading towards Dawn's house. As we got closer, we could see several more police cars that had surrounded her home. That was enough for me, and I started to turn around. I had seen all I needed to see. My worst fears were confirmed that Dawn had done exactly what Zach had originally said. Dawn had attempted suicide.

Upon returning home, I learned that I had missed two or three phone calls from friends who undoubtedly had called to tell me the news of Dawn's attempted suicide. The question that still remained for me was whether or not she had succeeded in killing herself. I did not want to call my friends back for fear of learning the answer to that question. As it turned out, I never would have gotten the chance anyway. Within minutes, two of my friends had arrived to deliver the news. Dawn was dead.

After talking for 10 minutes in the front yard, my friends left and my mother had returned home from the store. For approximately the next half hour, my mother and I talked about Dawn's suicide. We spoke only briefly about my conversation with Dawn on the bus ride home.

During our discussion, I remembered that I had choir practice at the university. Our high school concert choir was to rehearse for a May concert that was to take place soon. My mom mentioned that I did not have to go if I didn't want to. I replied by telling her that it would make me feel better to be around my friends instead of being cooped up at home.

At the rehearsal in the grand auditorium, I was surprised to see most if not all of the students carrying on as usual. I couldn't believe it. I was stunned. "They don't know yet, they don't know about Dawn's suicide," I thought to myself.

Surveying the room, I spotted Scott and Vicki near the top row of seating. Vicki was a senior whom I did not know very well, but Scott, also a senior, was a friend of mine who lived just down the street from me. I slowly began to climb the stairs to join them. As I got closer, Scott must have sensed that something was wrong.

"What's wrong, Doug?" he asked.

After taking a seat next to him, I simply shrugged my shoulders, looked at the floor, and answered, "Dawn is dead."

I'm sure they were startled. They heard me, but I'm not entirely sure they knew who I was talking about. After all, Scott and Vicki were seniors and Dawn and I were sophomores, and the concert choir consisted of dozens of students.

"What?" Scott asked, as if he might have misunderstood me.

"Dawn is dead. She killed herself," I answered.

Scott's jaw dropped for a moment, and then he turned to exchange looks with Vicki. After a few moments, Scott responded with typical youthful sarcasm.

"That sucks, Dude."

I instantly turned away. I wasn't upset, but I felt that Scott had trivialized the news of Dawn's suicide. He quickly noticed and put his arm around me, apologizing. He remembered how close Dawn and I had been, and he began trying to console me.

After a minute or two, I began to notice the scene below us changing. Somehow, the word was beginning to spread. The rehearsal hall was quickly becoming a place of shock and sadness. Then Mrs. Carroll, a school counselor, arrived and began discussing Dawn's suicide. I was not interested in listening to her try to explain to people what had happened to Dawn. I knew what had happened. I knew better than Mrs. Carroll did.

It was only hours ago that I had had the last conversation with Dawn. I was reliving the entire conversation in my head. With Mrs. Carroll's voice in the background, I couldn't stand it anymore and I rushed out of the room into the corridor.

I stared out of the window of the door and into the sunlight that was fading quickly into the coming night. Reflecting on the conversation I had earlier with Dawn, I had not noticed that I was no longer alone. I was startled by a voice coming from the other side of the corridor.

"How are you doing, Doug?"

It was Scott's friend, Vicki. I was surprised to see her since I hardly knew her. I tried to focus on her question and debated whether to say "Fine," or "Okay," which is what everybody says, but I was neither fine nor okay.

I did not answer Vicki's question right away. I was trying to decide whether or not to share my thoughts and feelings with her. I didn't know her well, I thought, but maybe that was the reason I decided to open up to her. She wouldn't judge me or look down at me for what I might say to her. Whatever the reason, I began to discuss my relationship with Dawn and what had happened between Dawn and me earlier that day.

As I began to speak, my emotions took over and I began to cry uncontrollably. Vicki quickly came to my side and sat me down. She said nothing. She only put her arms around me and tried to calm me down. After a few minutes, I was able to pull myself together enough to continue our conversation. I realized that it was the first time that I had cried for Dawn. What I didn't realize was that it would be a long time before I would shed any tears for Dawn again.

I turned my tearstained face and attention back to Vicki and looked her right in her face.

"I think I might have killed her," I confided.

I could see Vicki's demeanor change in a hurry. She looked a little more than somewhat surprised at my remark.

"It's not what you think, but it might as well be," I quickly added, wanting to put her at ease.

I began to tell her about the conversation Dawn and I had during the ride home on the bus. As Vicki listened, she became emotional, as well. She began to realize exactly why I was having such a hard time. Not only had I lost a friend, but I was feeling responsible. I have to admit I was scared. I didn't know how Vicki would view what I was telling her. I truly felt that I had talked Dawn into ending her own life, and now I was scared that Vicki might also believe that I was responsible for Dawn's suicide. I didn't expect her to come right out and say it, but I knew that I would be able to tell by her expressions. I was gauging Vicki's reaction to see how anyone else would react if they, too, knew of my conversation with Dawn.

I worried that my friends and Dawn's family might blame me. I wished for another chance to have that conversation on the bus ride home. I thought of all the things I would have said differently to Dawn. I wouldn't have glamorized Kevin's death as I had. I would have done the opposite. I would have pointed out what a poor choice Kevin made and how suicide only creates more problems and solves none.

Vicki began shaking her head back and forth, saying that I was not responsible for Dawn's death. While that was probably what I expected her to say, it was also what I needed to hear.

"A person does not decide to commit suicide based on a single conversation or based on the opinion of one person's beliefs of the afterlife," Vicki explained.

As our conversation continued and as an occasional student walked by, I experienced a strange feeling of déjà vu. I suddenly found myself having the same conversation with Vicki that I had had with Dawn—but this time the roles were reversed. I only wished I had been as effective with Dawn as Vicki was with me. Her words of comfort and understanding helped me through one of the lowest points in my life. Here was a near stranger giving me some comfort and peace. Our conversation was brief, but I would consider it one of the most important and unforgettable conversations I would ever have. Since that day, I'm sure Vicki has been many things to many people, but on that day, she was an angel to me.

At the conclusion of our talk, Vicki and I began to walk back into the main auditorium where Mrs. Carroll was still speaking with those students who had just learned of Dawn's suicide. I still have the vision of her standing in front of the piano with a pen in her hand and her face conveying the seriousness of the situation. Her voice was steady and firm.

As some were listening intently, hanging on every word, others were in small groups, huddling and crying. Others who did not know Dawn were still in amazement and sat quietly and simply surveyed the room, which was fully engulfed with emotions ranging from shock and sadness to bewilderment. I could hear some students saying that they couldn't take it anymore. Others could be heard saying, "First Kevin and now Dawn."

When Vicki and I returned to our seats, Scott was still where we'd left him.

"You all right?" Scott asked.

This time, Scott spoke with more sensitivity. I know that he felt bad about the way he had reacted earlier, and I wanted him to know that I wasn't angry with him.

"I'm fine. Don't worry about it," I said.

"Sorry about before," he continued.

"No need," I assured him.

It was becoming clear that rehearsal for the night was not going to take place. Parents of some of the students were already arriving to collect their sons and daughters. While some left, others remained. I suppose they did not want to go home and sit alone or talk to their parents about feelings that they themselves had not yet figured out.

It is curious that young people in high school sometimes wait to see how others form opinions before they develop their own. In any case, I stayed and observed the scene for a little longer until a few other friends came and invited me to another friend's house to hang out. My mind immediately went into reverse. I had done this before! I envisioned a group of my friends sitting around the room, crying and hugging, and I had no interest in doing that. I felt that Dawn would have liked that kind of attention, and I did not want to give it to her. I responded firmly, no.

Scott agreed to take me home, and as we reached the exit of the auditorium, I turned around to take a last look and thought to myself, "Good, I'm glad I'm leaving this emotional scene." My feelings were beginning to change about Dawn as they had for Kevin—from sadness to anger. And I certainly had no interest in reliving such an emotional roller coaster of sharing stories of Dawn at someone's house. I just wanted to go home.

My parents were sitting in the living room when I walked in. They asked me if I was all right, but I'm not sure they believed me because they forced me to sit down and said that they had some things that they wanted to discuss. Apparently, they had been on the phone with some other parents and Mrs. Carroll. It was then that I found out it was my mother who first called Mrs. Carroll about Dawn's death.

Neither of my parents came right out and said it, but they were concerned that perhaps I, too, had contemplated suicide. After shaking my head and making a few sloughing noises, I said they had nothing to worry about. I am not sure there was anything I could have said that would have satisfied them. They only kept repeating how worried they were. Each of them told me how much they loved me, and I went upstairs to bed. Looking back, I now realize just how lucky I was to have two parents who loved me and cared as much as they did.

As I sat alone in my bedroom, I reflected. What had started as a day in which I was trying to put Kevin's suicide and chaos behind me had ended with more chaos and yet another friend's suicide. I remember lying awake in bed and thinking back to the events of the day and of the week. Thoughts about the first day back to school after Kevin's death came to me.

I could remember the huddling at the lockers, the crying and hugging, and the grief counselors wandering through the hallways. There were also the countless hours of gathering at each other's houses and time we spent at the funeral home, auditorium, and the cemetery. I could even remember staring at the flag at half-mast in front of the high school. I remember it all, and I know that Dawn had remembered it, too.

How could Dawn commit suicide? I kept asking myself. Dawn saw all of the pain that Kevin's suicide caused her friends and family. Had she wanted everyone to be in more pain? Was it a way to be more popular after seeing how popular Kevin became after committing suicide? She knew there were unanswered questions concerning Kevin's death. Why had Kevin killed himself? She knew that none of us had the answer, so why, why would Dawn deliberately raise more questions and create more pain by committing the same horrible act? My anger was building.

I spent hours that night trying to answer that question. What possibly could have been bothering Dawn so much that she would end her own life? It couldn't have been her schoolwork. Dawn might not have had the highest grades in her class, but I always thought of her as a fairly good student, and her grades reflected that. I had heard that Dawn had recently been cut from next year's varsity football cheerleading squad, and I knew that she had struggled with the whole "being popular" thing, but we all go through that, and she certainly had a well-rounded group of friends.

Of course, there were the usual teen dilemmas—whether or not to drink, to smoke, or to have sex—but we all go through that, I thought. It couldn't have been Kevin. Dawn and Kevin were friends but not in a way that Dawn just couldn't go on without him. What could have been so troubling to her that she felt she could not share it with me or another friend? Why was suicide the only answer for her? That was all. I couldn't think of anything else in Dawn's life that would cause her to feel suicide was the only solution.

I began to replay the conversation that we had on the bus ride home. It was becoming clear to me that most of my anger toward Dawn was coming from the feeling that she had used me. I believe that Dawn had already decided to end her life prior to our conversation. However, I also believe that one hurdle still remained. Dawn struggled with the idea of Kevin being in hell for committing suicide. Maybe that explained the look on her face when I got on the bus. Maybe she was trying to decide if she wanted to take the chance of going to hell for committing the same act as Kevin. For Dawn, that's where I came in. She was trying to erase any lingering doubt about her decision to kill herself. She used me—someone that she trusted—to do that for her.

Dawn and I were having two totally different conversations. I was trying to help her feel better about Kevin's suicide and to assure her that he was not suffering in the flames of hell, whereas Dawn was using our conversation as a way to convince herself to commit suicide. I also remembered the strange question Dawn had asked me before I left her at her house, "Do you want to come in and talk more about suicide or do something about it?"

Dawn's comment "or do something about it" haunted me. I didn't catch it at the time. Had I known what we were truly talking about, I would never have left her alone that day. I never dreamed that she could be at risk of ending her life! Unfortunately, when she invited me to come inside, I said, No.

I kept telling myself repeatedly that I was not trying to romanticize or glamorize Kevin's act of suicide, only trying to make Dawn feel better. Why couldn't she see that? I had been oblivious to her pain, to her intent, and that bothered me most of all.

The next morning, I got ready for school as always. After grabbing some breakfast, I started out the door. My mom asked me if I wanted to stay home that day and offered to stay with me. This was highly unusual because my mother never let my brother or me stay home, even if we had a 104-degree temperature. I assured her that I was okay, but in retrospect, she was probably afraid that I would commit suicide, also, and she would never see me again after I left the house.

While riding on the bus to school, I only heard one conversation that dealt with Dawn's suicide. For a moment, I was thinking that maybe we could all just move on with life and possibly not make Dawn's death a big deal as we had done with Kevin's. Or maybe I was just hoping. I do not mean to be insensitive, but I was adamant about not wanting to put Dawn on the pedestal that I felt we had placed Kevin on.

It didn't take long for me to realize that that was not going to happen. I was walking from the parking lot where the bus had let us off when I noticed Chuck, a friend of mine, and another friend lowering the flag again to half-mast.

"What are you doing?" I asked Chuck.

He looked surprised that I would even ask such a question. His face then turned calmer as he perhaps thought that I didn't know about Dawn's suicide.

"Dawn died last night," Chuck replied, trying to explain the situation.

"You just don't get it, do you?" I said, mumbling to myself, then turning from him to enter the building.

Entering the doorway, I thought to myself, Dawn took this same walk into the high school a week ago. She saw all of the attention Kevin received, and I know she saw how much more popular Kevin became in the wake of his suicide. Since his death, he had been the talk of the town. Come to think about it, Kevin was still being talked about the day that Dawn committed suicide.

I thought back to Kevin's funeral arrangements. His visitation was well attended, the line was long at the funeral home, the flag at the school was at half-mast, and his funeral was like a damn assembly at the junior high auditorium, for crying out loud!

The events and our actions since Kevin's suicide had been to honor his memory. Not once had I heard any of my friends say that Kevin made a bad decision. The more I thought about it, the more I realized that we had honored Kevin and had set him on some pedestal like a god. What some of us had actually done was glamorize

Kevin's death. It was easy. I had done it myself just hours earlier in my conversation with Dawn.

I wish I could have seen what we were doing, but I didn't. I just kept replaying the conversation on the bus over and over again in my mind. I was guilty in the entire conversation; I had glamorized suicide and probably made it look like an option for all of Dawn's problems. It never entered my mind that Dawn, or any of us, was in any danger. I guess I just felt that what had happened to Kevin was an isolated incident, and nobody else would suffer his same fate.

I didn't know that Dawn or Kevin were so deeply depressed. I didn't know Dawn was thinking of taking her own life. I didn't know that she was debating the issue of the afterlife. I just didn't know. I became angrier and angrier for not seeing what was really going on.

After entering the building, I bypassed my locker and walked straight into Mrs. Carroll's office. She was talking to a grief counselor when I arrived. I must have interrupted their conversation, but at the time, I didn't care.

"Why is the flag being lowered to half-mast?" I asked.

I raised my voice to be sure that I had their attention. The two of them stopped talking and just looked at me. After a brief pause, they looked at each other, and then Mrs. Carroll turned to me and said,

"I'm sure they just want to show respect over Dawn's death."

I turned and began to walk out, again mumbling under my breath, "She didn't just die. She *killed herself.*"

As I left the office and went to my locker, I decided at that moment that I would not tell anyone about the conversation I had with Dawn on the bus the day before. I also had decided that I would not attend any visitation, any service, and I would discuss Dawn's suicide with as few people as possible. My plan was to mourn privately.

I was not going to contribute to any more glorification of someone's poor choices.

Later that day, I was called down to the guidance office by Mrs. Carroll. She sat me down and began to discuss Dawn's suicide in a seemingly one-sided conversation, trying to make me feel comfortable. I respected Mrs. Carroll because she'd been my English teacher in seventh grade, and I had always liked her and regarded her as one of my favorite teachers. I also knew that she was always looking out for me. Therefore, while I meant no disrespect, I did not want to discuss Kevin's or Dawn's suicide with her or anyone else.

Nevertheless, she was determined to try to help me even though her help was unwelcome. She explained that she was worried not only because she knew I was close to Kevin and Dawn, but because of my outburst that morning in the presence of the grief counselor. I quickly apologized for that, but that was not enough. Unknown to me, she had spoken with my mother and they had both decided that I needed to speak with someone. She was going to have me sit with a group of friends and talk with a grief counselor from the Children's Resource Center (CRC). Realizing that I had never won an argument with Mrs. Carroll and that I wasn't going to win this one either, I agreed.

Shortly thereafter, I met with some of my friends and Bill, the grief counselor from CRC, at a table in the back of the library. He started by having us tell him how we all knew Dawn.

All I remember of the meeting was that some cried and sobbed and others just spoke of the devastation that they felt from losing another classmate. As for me, I said practically nothing. I was still being a little stubborn and stuck to my guns about not discussing Dawn's suicide anymore. Maybe I was still feeling guilty because I had failed miserably in my attempt to help Dawn and I didn't feel like talking about it again with anybody else. I also felt that we might be giving suicide more undeserved attention, and we could again be inadvertently contributing to someone else's thoughts of suicide.

Dawn meant a lot to me, but I truly did believe that the attention given to Kevin's suicide contributed to her decision to kill herself—or at the very least, it made her feel that she wasn't alone in her decision. I felt it was possible that Kevin had unknowingly given her strength to carry out what she already wanted to do. And as for me, I started to worry that if I were to talk about it with someone else, I may inadvertently convince that person to do it as well. So my mind was made up. I was not going to talk about it anymore to anyone, and certainly not to a friend or fellow classmate.

The meeting continued with my classmates discussing the tragedy and expressing their pain. After approximately an hour, the meeting began to break up and Bill asked me to stay for a while and talk with him. My first notion was to say no, but I knew that would probably only raise more flags, so I agreed. I had this sense that I was being pegged as one of those kids who didn't talk about feelings, didn't want to confront feelings, and therefore, was a risk to commit suicide as well. The only request that I had was that we speak in private. I did not want any of my classmates to see me talking with a grief counselor. I did not want to be labeled as a "nut job" or as someone just trying to get attention.

Bill accommodated me, and we slipped back into Mrs. Carroll's office, which was vacant at the time. He started by stating that he had heard that I was close to Dawn and that Mrs. Carroll was worried about me. He then attempted to ease any tension that may have existed in the conversation by letting me know that he was not there to judge me or force anything on me, only that he, too, was concerned, and that he had noticed that I was silent during the group meeting. He thought I might be more comfortable talking in a one-on-one setting.

I was beginning to realize that if I wanted this meeting to end, I was going to have to participate in it. Therefore, I decided to give the guy a break and talk with him. I told myself that if talking with Bill would put everyone at ease, then I would do so. I also would allow myself to speak with Bill about the conversation on the bus and my relationship with Dawn. Bill seemed harmless, and if I were going to talk about Dawn's suicide, I would have to include everything.

I began by letting Bill know that I was not at risk of committing suicide. I'm sure that was on his mind. It was no surprise that one of the main topics in the hallways at school was, "Who's going to be next? First Kevin, then Dawn." It wasn't crazy to think that there might be an epidemic starting at our high school. All of us had heard stories of other places across America where there had been copycat suicides.

I told Bill that I didn't believe in or subscribe to either of my friends' decisions to end their own lives. I explained to him how Kevin's death confused and saddened me. I spoke of all the emotions that I had gone through during Kevin's death. Then I spoke of the differences, as I saw them, between Kevin's and Dawn's suicides.

I also told him of my anger toward Dawn, that I had no interest in going to any service or funeral that would take place for her. I would not contribute to Dawn's poor decision of taking her own life by attending her funeral. I was mad! I explained to him that I felt Dawn knew better than Kevin did after seeing how a suicide can affect family and friends. She saw all of the pain that Kevin created, and she knew that killing herself would create the same attention and pain. I went on to explain that I could not help thinking that she was okay with this knowledge. I didn't believe that Dawn was trying to get even with anyone, only that she was depressed and wanted out. If people grieved for her at the same time, then, in her mind, that would be icing on the cake.

In addition, I spoke of the mistakes I believed the school was making as it pertained to the suicide of Kevin and now of Dawn. I told him how I felt about all of the attention and "celebrity status" that was—and is—currently taking place. I did not stop there either; suddenly, I went from not wanting to talk to anyone to spilling my guts with feelings of sorrow, pain, anger, guilt, and frustration.

I pointed to the "glamour" of having the school flag at half-mast, the counselors in the halls, the crying at the lockers, the huddling together at friends' houses, and all of the attention that we were giving to two people who had made the worst choice of their lives. During the conversation with Bill, I began thinking and then voicing the words:

"If they don't want to be a part of my life anymore, then I don't want to be a part of theirs."

I found Bill easy to talk to, and I genuinely felt better after our conversation. He proved to be an effective sounding board, and his advice was sterling.

I needed to talk with an objective person—like Vicki—a person who would not judge me or my feelings. He didn't even have to understand everything that I was feeling. He just needed to listen and not try to tell me what was best for me or to tell me how to grieve. I thanked Bill, but as I walked out of the office and started back to class, I knew that I would not speak of Dawn's suicide again to Bill or to anyone else, at least, not if I could help it.

Later that evening when I had the conversation with my mother about not wanting to go to Dawn's visitation or funeral, she expressed some of the concerns and had some of the same questions that Mrs. Carroll and

Bill had. Wanting to avoid having the same conversation with my mom that I'd had earlier had with Bill, I simply provided her with some generic answers that she would accept. My mother had no problem with my not attending. She just wanted to make sure that I was choosing not to go for the right reasons. After convincing her that I just wanted to move on, she agreed.

As Dawn's visitation and funeral neared, my classmates and friends behaved emotionally, as one would expect. Dawn's close friends, and even those who did not know her, huddled and behaved as though their world was crashing in around them. I always chuckled disgustedly at those who never gave Dawn the time of day when she was alive, but now they behaved as if they had lost the best friend of their life.

It was one of the bitter lessons I would learn through the experience of losing classmates. Generally, everyone wants to be included in the attention that follows—something that would dissipate as quickly as it materialized. As the wind changes, so does the mind of an adolescent.

Both the visitation and the funeral came and went without my attendance. I went to my grandmother's house for the weekend to escape the sad scene. While I put on a good show in front of my family, there wasn't a minute that went by that I didn't think of Dawn, Kevin, and how the scene of Dawn's funeral was surely transpiring. I remember feeling lucky that I was able to escape the tearful event. I meant no disrespect. I just felt emotionally exhausted.

CHAPTER 3

Samantha

It was the following spring, 1988. The anniversary of Kevin's and Dawn's suicides was approaching quickly. It was hard to believe that it had already been a year since their suicides, and, unless you lived in a box, you knew of the approaching anniversary.

It is customary for people to mark the anniversary of loved ones that have died. When I was 11 years old (the same year Harry died), I lost two aunts and a cousin in the span of 3 months. To this day, there isn't a summer that passes in which I don't remember their deaths.

Marking the suicidal deaths of my friends on the calendar felt different, though. It brought one of the darkest times in my life back to the front of my mind. You could almost feel the wind of emotion from others in the school as the dates approached. It was a cold and unwelcome wind, however.

I didn't want to go through those painful emotions again. Their suicides still scared me and reminded me of a time that made me unsure of myself and of the world around me. I had searched to find answers to the questions that remained, and when I couldn't find them, I simply made them up. I had to. I had to find a way to move forward, and I had no interest in reliving the dark past. "They chose to commit suicide. They chose not to be here," I thought to myself.

Nevertheless, anniversaries of tragedies receive almost as much attention as birthdays and weddings, or at least for a while. Typically, a church service or some sort of gathering marks the anniversary of a death. Eventually, it is only the family who mourn the loss. For everyone else, the loss only becomes a memory that we reflect upon and shake our head in sad remembrance.

This is especially true if we lose a friend in our youth. In time, the pain moves further and further to the back of our minds because we become consumed with living. We go on to college or join the workforce, we have families of our own, and we make house and car payments. We live life. Only on a few occasions do we look at the calendar and feel the pain that we felt when the event was fresh to us.

I personally have mixed feelings about marking the anniversary of a death by suicide. I worry that we will mistakenly glamorize the manner of death instead of memorializing the person. In addition, I especially worry about a young person who remembers a friend's suicide and views that decision as an option for solving their own problems.

I had no such problem with the 1-year anniversary of Kevin's and Dawn's suicides. I still felt much of the anger that I harbored towards both of them, and, therefore, I had made the decision not to attend any service or gathering. On the other hand, it was impossible to escape all of the attention the anniversaries were generating, and I also would be unable to escape my feelings for Kevin and Dawn.

I was still angry, but I also missed both of them. I missed the "guy stuff" with Kevin, and I missed talking to Dawn. They were two of my best friends, and their suicides were back on the front page of conversation. Anytime I heard their names or heard about the anniversary of their suicides, I would think to myself, "Hope it was worth it, guys."

Since their deaths, each day brought more healing than the one before it. I moved on as well as I could and tried to stay busy. I avoided huddling in groups and discussing their deaths, and I avoided going to the cemetery where they were buried. Because of my anger towards Dawn, I had vowed not to go and visit. I still felt that I would somehow be honoring her decision to kill herself and giving her exactly what she wanted, attention and pity, and I refused.

During one spring day at school (the thoughts of the 1-year anniversary still fresh), I began to pack up my things in anticipation of the last bell. I remember bending down and stuffing papers and folders into my book bag when I heard a classmate of mine run past the room yelling, "No! No! No!" Right away, the mouse in my head started running. My mind quickly began to believe that another person had possibly committed suicide.

"That's crazy," I thought to myself.

We were in school. These things happen at home or somewhere else. They certainly don't happen here. I glanced around the room to see if there was any other reaction to what I had just heard from the hallway. To my amazement, there were only a couple of students next to me who seemed to have heard the yelling.

"I'm crazy. No need to panic," I said in a whispered voice that only I could hear.

Even so, I could not stop wondering if I were crazy, or if the next shoe was about to drop. As the bell rang and we began to file out, however, that scenario changed. News travels fast. As soon as I walked out of the room, I looked down the hall and saw three students huddled in front of their lockers, crying and embracing one another.

Immediately, I headed directly to the main office. I was looking for Mrs. Carroll to see what was going on. On my way, I saw only a few students looking somewhat shocked and getting emotional. Most of the student body was carrying on as usual, but I could feel that something was wrong.

I took a couple of steps into the main office and surveyed the room. There didn't appear to be anything out of the ordinary. Other than a couple of students and staff milling around, all seemed normal. I took a closer look around as I was searching for Mrs. Carroll. Then I saw two girls, classmates of mine, in a room adjoining the main office. Both girls were sitting at a table with a box of tissues, crying and clinging to one another. I didn't know them personally, but I recognized both of them as classmates. I stared at them for a second and began to fear the worst.

Turning my attention to the office secretary, I asked where I could find Mrs. Carroll. The secretary and I did not know one another, but I knew that she recognized me as one of the students that had struggled with the suicides of Kevin and Dawn.

Before she had a chance to answer, the door to the principal's office swung open and a police officer walked out. That was all I needed to see to convince me that something was wrong. I could only fear that another classmate had at least tried to commit suicide. I turned my focus toward the secretary and asked again, this time more forcefully,

"Where is Mrs. Carroll?"

She paused again but replied that Mrs. Carroll had stepped out. I turned my head again to the two girls sitting in the room. I stared at them once more, but only for a moment. I quickly turned to leave the office as I heard the secretary call after me loudly that I could wait for Mrs. Carroll in the office. I ignored her suggestion and continued out into the hall.

I looked both ways down the hallway and noticed a commotion in the vicinity of the gymnasium. Police officers were moving about. I made my way briskly to the far end of the corridor to an open door exiting to the outside from which vantage point I could see the track, police, fire and rescue personnel, etc. I then spotted Mrs. Carroll coming back toward the school with a police officer. She saw me and asked me to join her in her office.

On my way into the office, the secretary and I exchanged glances and then I again saw the two girls in the adjoining room attempting to comfort each other. I decided to sit in the chair nearest to the hallway. I still wasn't sure what had really happened yet. All I could figure out by my own observations was that apparently another student had attempted suicide. A steady stream of law enforcement persons and emergency medical persons, teachers, and counselors came and went. I tried to listen carefully to pick up any clues as to what had happened and to whom. Then I overheard one teacher telling another that Tracy Flockencier, one of the school's physical education teachers, had found her. I know I must have raised my eyebrows when I heard the comment. I thought, "Oh my god, someone hanged themselves in school." They said they had "found her."

It was a girl. Then I heard the same teacher mention that she had shot herself! I couldn't believe what I had just heard. A fellow student had shot herself—at school!

The two teachers left the office almost as fast as they had come in. I looked at the secretary and quietly asked her,

"Who . . . ?"

"I don't know the girl's name," the secretary answered.

"So it was a girl?" I asked as if I were some sort of detective.

"I think so, but that's all I know." Her tone indicated that she did not want me to ask any more questions. I won't forget her face as she spoke to me. She was as freaked out as I was. It was then that I realized how the suicides were affecting our teachers and staff. I never really gave any of them a second thought. I was so consumed with my own grief and that of my friends that I had not noticed.

While I sat in the chair still waiting for Mrs. Carroll to come out and talk with me, I began to feel sick to my stomach. And the more I waited, the sicker I felt. My body became cold, and my skin felt as if spiders were crawling on it. The flashbacks started. I shuddered at the idea of being forced to relive the past. I feared that we again would make the mistake of glorifying those who had made a bad decision. I kept feeling sicker at the idea of reliving these emotions again.

It was the copycat suicide that I feared the most. "It only takes one," I thought to myself. It was the attention that a teen suicide brings to a school that is our enemy. I tried to climb into the brain of a depressed teenager to try to understand the thought process.

If someone is already depressed and searching for answers, then the suicide of a friend could be viewed as a solution to their problems—especially if the suicide is attended by an undue amount of attention, and the attention is simply the icing on the cake, just as I thought Dawn had believed.

Or maybe it's the feeling of having the last word: "They will be sorry once I'm gone, and then they will understand just how bad it was for me."

Alternatively, some people will convince themselves of the lie: "Everyone would just be better off if I weren't here anymore."

I could say a lot concerning these two lies, but I will simply say that through my experience, a suicide victim never has the last word. I have had lots of words with my two friends Kevin and Dawn. It's a shame that they will never be around to hear any of them.

Finally, the door to the principal's office opened, and Mrs. Carroll emerged. As soon as she spotted me, she came to where I was sitting.

"I'm sorry, Doug. Time got away from me, and I forgot that you were out here waiting."

"No problem," I said, standing up to follow Mrs. Carroll to her office.

I was very anxious to find out who had shot herself and when. I sat down in the chair across from her desk and can remember praying that it wasn't someone that I knew. I know it sounds terrible, just looking out for my own feelings and not wanting the suicide victim to be someone that I was close to, but I wasn't sure if I could handle losing another friend or acquaintance to suicide.

"Doug, we had another student attempt suicide," Mrs. Carroll began.

"Attempt?" I asked, surprised.

Mrs. Carroll did not know that I had already overheard a couple of teachers commenting on a girl shooting herself. I could not imagine that someone had shot himself or herself and survived.

"That's right. Samantha shot herself outdoors near the track," she replied.

"Samantha? But she's not dead?" I asked.

"No, she's not dead, but she is in critical condition at the hospital. Did you know Samantha?" she asked.

"No, I didn't really know her," I answered.

I couldn't even picture what she looked like. I didn't know her, I thought to myself, and embarrassed to be relieved. I was sure Kevin and Dawn did not know her either, or at least as far as I knew they did not. But that was the point. This event could not be confused as part of a reaction by a person who was just too broken up to go on without Kevin and Dawn.

Samantha was obviously another person who bought into the lie that she was alone in this world, and that her problems were too large to handle. So in a final attempt to solve her problems, she had put a gun to her head and pulled the trigger.

"Jesus!" I blurted aloud. "Is this what we do now?" I said.

Mrs. Carroll just stared at me with a confused look on her face.

"We just kill ourselves when things aren't going our way," I continued.

I could tell that Mrs. Carroll was becoming mentally exhausted. Anyone could certainly understand. She had come to work that day and had now found herself in the middle of another possible suicide.

I am sure that she was also fully aware of what the future would bring in light of yet another suicide, and now she had what seemed to be a hysterical kid in her office that she had to deal with gently out of fear of what possibly he might do to himself. I was just about to cut her a break and ease her mind before I left when she broke the silence.

"Doug, I'm worried about you—and the whole school, for that matter—but I know you had a hard time dealing with losing your friends last year and I want to make sure that you're going to be okay."

"I'm sorry, I know you have people to see and meetings and stuff. I'm fine. Don't worry," I replied, sorry that I had even brought any more burdens to her plate.

"Don't worry about any of that stuff . . . and you know I'm not letting you leave until I'm satisfied anyway, so why don't we talk for a few moments," she demanded.

I felt bad about even coming in, but I knew Mrs. Carroll wasn't kidding about not letting me leave, so I began. I started to explain how I believed Kevin must have had some deep depression and felt no way out. I had no idea where Kevin came up with his plan of suicide, but he obviously felt he had to get out of his life.

Dawn was no doubt depressed, but I was certain that she had felt some comfort with the idea that she was not alone in deciding to end her own life. And then there was Samantha, whom I did not know, attempting to end her life with a gun.

"Have we all just gone nuts?" I said, looking at Mrs. Carroll.

I could tell by her expression that I may have been worrying her with the passion in my voice, or maybe I was convincing her that I was not an at-risk suicidal kid. I could not be sure. In any case, I remember putting my hands up and saying.

"I'm fine."

Just then, I could hear some commotion outside Mrs. Carroll's door. More people were coming out of the principal's office, and I knew that Mrs. Carroll probably had to go. I looked her straight in the eyes and said, "I'll be fine. I'm going to call my mom and get a ride home."

She asked me if I was sure. I replied that I was and mentioned that I would stop in tomorrow so that she could see for herself.

"Okay, Doug, I'm counting on you. Don't let me down."

And with that, she walked out of her office and into another for her next meeting. She was a rock—a true rock for all of us who had the pleasure to know her.

I walked out of the office, knowing that I had just lied to Mrs. Carroll. Yes, I was going to be okay, but I was not going to call my mom for a ride home. My mom worked about a half hour from where we lived and would not be on her way home for at least another 2 hours.

There was nobody to take me home, and I did not want Mrs. Carroll to feel obligated to take me herself. Besides, there would be nobody but me at home, and I knew she would never drop me off at an empty house after what had just happened again at school. How could I blame her? I wouldn't feel comfortable dropping off a kid whose friends had killed themselves a year ago and then just talked to him about another attempted suicide.

I wanted to walk home anyway. I could use the fresh air and the exercise. I remember leaving the school by an alternate route so that Mrs. Carroll could not see me from her office window. On the way home, I was thinking about Samantha and also about the events of the past year. I could not help wondering if Kevin and Dawn had anything to do with Samantha trying to end her life. I was shaking my head in despair during the walk home, wondering if Samantha was still an "attempted" suicide or if she had now joined Kevin and Dawn as a suicide statistic.

Would Samantha be the last—the last this year to attempt or commit suicide? I thought it was over with Kevin. I never gave it a second thought. Then I was at least hoping that it was over with Dawn. I couldn't imagine that we hadn't learned our lesson. Nevertheless, there I was, walking home, shaking my head, dreading the loss of another classmate, and praying that this would certainly be the last suicidal tragedy.

Later that night, when both my mom and dad got home, I told them about Samantha shooting herself at school on the track. I vividly remember my dad's reaction.

"Geez!" he said, with a surprised look on his face.

My mom simply stood there with her mouth open.

"Did you know her?" Mom asked.

"No, I didn't know her," I replied.

I gave them the details and said that Samantha was alive, at least at the time I had left school. Now both of their mouths seemed to hit the floor.

"She shot herself *at school*?" my mom asked.

"Yes," I repeated.

"My god! You okay?" my dad asked.

"Yeah, I'm fine," I answered.

"You didn't know her, though?" Mom asked again.

"No," I answered, a little annoyed by the same questions over and over.

I could tell that they were shaken. After all, we had had another suicide, or attempted suicide, and no one knew if Samantha was alive or dead. My parents continued to repeat themselves, probably because they did not know what else to say or ask. I tried to mitigate their anxiety by saying that I did not know Samantha, hoping to soften the blow a bit. Still, I was totally freaked out by Samantha's attempted suicide AT SCHOOL—and WITH A GUN!

"School is supposed to be a place safe from violence," I protested.

Later that night, Zach, from down the road—the one who was a junior high student during the time of Kevin's and Dawn's suicides—called to talk about Samantha's suicide attempt. He had heard that a girl shot and killed herself on the track at the high school. I told him that as far as I knew, Samantha was still alive. I was in awe of the speed with which information travels.

My phone conversation with Zach, however, did prompt me to once again wonder what Samantha's condition might be. I thought of all the tubes and needles going in and out of her. I thought of the doctors and nurses fighting to keep her alive. I imagined the family grieving in the hallway of the hospital and wondering what went wrong. I pictured family members calling each other, saying, "If only Samantha had realized how important she is to people who love her. If only she had fought the urge to harm herself as much as she is now fighting to stay alive in that hospital room." Why must an event so tragic and drastic happen in order for us to understand how much we mean to our loved ones?

If Samantha died, I knew exactly what to expect the next day, and I dreaded that her suicide would receive attention. There would undoubtedly be students who knew her well, huddling and crying by their lockers, and there would be grief counselors roaming the halls, but I wondered if we had learned anything from the last year's suicides, and I wondered if we would repeat the mistake of making Samantha a martyr and glamorizing a bad decision.

Walking into school the next morning, I noticed the flag was still at full mast, so I thought to myself, "Either she's not dead, or the school has gotten smarter." I entered the building and started down the hallway. I did not stop to talk to anyone and nothing seemed out of ordinary. I had yet to hear a word of yesterday's suicide attempt.

Upon reaching my locker, I unloaded my books, grabbed what I needed for my first class, and walked to the cafeteria, where I visited with friends before school started. It was much different from the scene a year ago when Dawn and Kevin killed themselves. I was beginning to think that I had imagined Samantha shooting herself the day before, but as I approached the table where my friends were sitting, I could hear them talking about the girl that had shot herself. I sat down across the table from my friend Todd, who was doing most of the talking.

"Doug, did you hear about the girl that shot herself yesterday?" he inquired.

"Yes, but I didn't hear whether or not she died," I added.

"She's alive, Dude," he answered.

I was in total shock. When I had gone to bed the night before, I knew it was possible, but I really did not think Samantha could survive a gunshot wound to the head.

"You've got to be kidding me! Are you sure?" I asked.

"Yep, Miss Flockencier found that girl yesterday when she went out to set up for track practice," Todd continued.

Our conversation about the girl who shot herself continued as we walked to class, and I was feeling strange about all of us calling her "that girl," so I spoke up and mentioned that her name was Samantha.

"Do any of you know Samantha?" I asked.

"Who's Samantha?" Todd asked.

"The girl that shot herself," I answered. I was amazed that none of them knew her name.

"I didn't know her," another answered.

Everyone else just nodded in agreement. Others mentioned that they had not recognized her from the yearbook either.

"Do you sense that everybody is reacting differently today about Samantha than they did about Dawn and Kevin?" I asked Todd.

"Probably a little bit, but we didn't know her. Plus, I think everybody's just sick of the whole suicide thing," Todd tried to explain.

"I guess so, but it just seems different to me, as if nobody cares as much," I continued.

"I don't know. That girl didn't die either, Doug," Todd answered.

I started to remind Todd that her name was Samantha, but I didn't and I continued walking.

In first period class, we could overhear others in the room talking about Samantha being brain-dead or in a coma. I couldn't believe some of the claims that were being made. How would they know, I thought to myself.

She had shot herself only yesterday and even her own doctors wouldn't have some of the information that these people seemed to possess. It was amazing how people can sensationalize a tragedy. I started to chuckle to myself because here was a girl whose name we didn't even know a few minutes ago, and now we claimed to know every detail about her. What a farce, I thought!

The rumors continued throughout the day. Everybody had a version about what happened to Samantha. Speculation concerning her spread like wildfire, stories from what kind of gun she had used to all of the reasons that she shot herself. Again, I laughed at all of the information that poured from those who hardly knew her. It was amazing to me how many people claim to know a person after a tragedy has taken place.

I happened across Mrs. Carroll, who asked, "Are you okay? How are you doing?"

I answered jokingly, "Hey, I'm getting used to it."

I couldn't believe that I had just joked about Samantha's suicide attempt. Thankfully, Mrs. Carroll seemed to understand. She knew that I didn't mean anything by my comments.

"I'm sorry. I didn't mean any disrespect," I added immediately.

"It was bound to happen," she said.

I had been through just about every emotion you could think of the past year. I was so drained and mentally exhausted that making light of the tragedy seemed easier. It may sound crazy, but I actually think it made me feel better to joke about it. I don't necessarily recommend joking about a death, let alone a death by suicide, but I understand why some people do it. It is their way to deal with something they don't understand.

I asked Mrs. Carroll if there was any new news on Samantha's condition. Even though I did not know her, I was still concerned for Samantha's own personal well-being, concerned about the school coping with the loss of another student, and also concerned about other classmates who might be contemplating suicide themselves.

"She's still fighting for her life," Mrs. Carroll responded.

I couldn't help thinking that if only she had been fighting for her own life yesterday, she wouldn't have to fight so hard today.

"Could you keep me informed of any changes in Samantha's condition?" I asked.

"Will do," she nodded and walked away.

Later that night, I spent a lot of time trying to make sense out of suicide. I simply wanted to understand the act and the mental process that goes into making such a decision. I had been in school for 11 years and had never heard of anybody in our school committing suicide. I had heard of teen suicides in other communities but never in our own backyard. Maybe I thought the world was different where I lived.

Whatever it was, I had never given suicide a second thought, yet in a year's time, I was confronted with the suicidal deaths of two of my friends and also the suicide attempt of another classmate. I dreaded the phone ringing and the person on the line telling me that another friend was dead.

The end of the year came without any further suicides or suicide attempts. Samantha's condition did improve and after a long battle physically and mentally, she made it back to school. She walked with a cane and seemed to lose some control of her motor functions, but considering how far she had come, she was doing remarkably well.

A couple of months later, I attended the graduation ceremony as a member of the concert choir that performed each year. When the time came for the choir to assemble on the stage, I glanced to my right where Dawn would have been standing. It was difficult for me to look over and not see her.

It occurred to me that I truly would never see Dawn again. I found it difficult to concentrate. Dawn and I were supposed to be seniors. We used to talk about our senior year and how we were going to spend it. I knew at that moment that next year's graduation would be difficult for me.

After we had said our good-byes to the class of '88 and we were in the back room taking off our choir robes, the discussion turned to graduation parties and summer plans, but I couldn't stop thinking about all that had happened over the last year and what we had lost. I remember taking a moment to scan the room. As I watched everyone and listened to all of the different conversations that were taking place, I learned a valuable lesson: Life goes on.

I only wish that Harry, Kevin, Dawn, Samantha, and anyone else who has committed suicide (or tried to commit suicide) had learned that lesson *before* they ended their lives. If they had, they would have known that their lasting legacy with their friends from school would not amount to anything more than a "remember-when" story.

CHAPTER 4

An Accident

In 1991, 4 years after the suicides of Kevin and Dawn, I was attending college at Owens Community College in Toledo, was a member of the college baseball team, and was working part-time. I still had many of the same friends from high school and our routine hadn't changed too much from our days in high school. We spent the majority of our time on the weekends playing basketball at Old Man's Gym, which is what we called Eppler Gymnasium at Bowling Green State University. It formerly played host to all home university basketball games but more recently had been used for physical education classes, and on weeknights and weekends, it was a place for pickup basketball games.

While many of our other friends were out partying and drinking, Steve, Dave, Mike, Carl, Chris, my brother Jeff, and I were usually playing basketball at Old Man's Gym. Not that I was judging my friends who liked to party, but to me, it was never worth the risk of getting into trouble at home or with the law. Anyway, some or all of us played almost every weekend. We showed up, found out who had the next game, and waited in line. Winners always kept playing.

We weren't the only regulars at the gym. We got to know a lot of others whose age range included junior high kids to men over 50. For some, the purpose of playing was to stay young and in shape, and for others, the purpose was to practice and to help their game in high school.

Kevin, Shawn, Andy, Tony, and Jay were another group that we often saw at the gym. They were sophomores in high school, exactly the same age as I was when Kevin and Dawn committed suicide. They were all members of the basketball team and went to the gym to sharpen their skills against some older and more experienced competition. We knew these kids because all of them lived in the same city and were involved in many activities beyond basketball. All of them were hardworking kids who never got into any real trouble and were well respected throughout the community. While I knew all five from around town, I really got to know them best from the Old Man's Gym.

In 1991, a different type of tragedy struck our community. In March of that year, a car accident took the lives of four teenagers and injured a fifth.

Kevin, Maggie, Tina, and Stephanie were sophomores at the high school. Kevin played basketball at Old Man's Gym and was, at the time of the accident, a member of the high school baseball team. I also knew his father as one of the football coaches at the university.

A second victim of the crash was Maggie, whom I had known through friends that we mutually shared, and I also knew her father as my eleventh-grade history teacher.

Tina, the driver of the car, was the third victim who lost her life. I didn't know Tina at all and wasn't sure if I had ever met her. I would find out later that her father was a university professor.

Likewise, I had never met Stephanie, the fourth victim. I only knew her father from being involved in Little League baseball and softball.

Sara, a fifth passenger in the car, had escaped with injuries.

All five teenage passengers involved in the tragedy were well-known and respected members of the community. I knew that the aftermath of the accident would be very similar to the drama that I had witnessed during my sophomore and junior years at the high school. The major difference, of course, was that in the tragedies of '87, the victims chose self-destruction, whereas the victims of the car crash did not choose to die.

I was empathetic for those who were close to the victims and wished that I could take away the pain that they surely would go through. I knew what they were going to be feeling over the next few days, weeks, and months. For some, the pain would never completely go away. There is no pain greater than that of a young high school student losing a close friend.

After the tragedy, my friend Carl and I had decided to go to the funeral home to pay respects to Kevin and his family. As we arrived, we realized that the visitations for two of the victims, Kevin and Maggie, were occurring simultaneously. The number of people in attendance was staggering. The queue of mourners snaked from the doorway down the sidewalk to the street. It appeared that the entire high school of 1,200 and half of the community converged on one funeral home all at once. I had only witnessed a scene like this one other time. "Kevin," I thought to myself.

I instantly felt a lump in my throat as I walked closer to Kevin's family. Next to Kevin's body was his father, extending his hand to greet me. I had never met Kevin's dad before that day. I was amazed and struck by his emotional strength. He had lost his son only a couple of days ago and there he was, greeting over 1,000 people with such courage and dignity.

"I'm so sorry for your loss," I said to Kevin's dad.

"Thank you. How did you know him?" he asked.

"I played basketball with him at Old Man's Gym," I replied.

"He loved playing there," Kevin's dad said with finality in his voice, ending the conversation.

I continued down the line to have a moment at Kevin's body, and then Carl and I began to leave the funeral home. We were stopped at the door by a group of others who had come to pay their respects. We spoke briefly of memories about Kevin and the others that lost their lives in the accident.

I noticed Maggie's father in the other room. I wanted to let him know how sorry I was for his loss but was apprehensive about how it might be received. I don't know why I felt apprehensive, but I did. Maggie's father had been my American History teacher when I was a junior in high school. He was also responsible for my interest in history and my decision to major in that subject in college. I'm sure he never knew how influential he had been in my life. I had much respect for the man, and it was very difficult to see him coping with the loss of his daughter.

I excused myself from the group by the door and began to walk towards Maggie's father. As I approached, I froze. I found myself standing by a chair at the back of the room, just staring into space. I knew that Dawn had had her service at this same funeral home and began to wonder if this was the same room that she had been in. It had been 4 years, and I was still very upset with her and did not regret not attending her service. My feelings about her final decision were still very much the same.

"Doug?"

I heard my name called. I snapped out of whatever trance I was in and turned my attention to the voice. It was Maggie's father. He looked at me with a little surprise and curiosity.

"I just wanted to tell you how sorry I was about what happened," I answered.

I'm not sure how it happened, but I then found myself in an embrace and I began to cry. Looking back on that night at the funeral home, I believe my sadness for Maggie's father was only part of the reason I became so emotional. I had had Dawn on my mind that entire day. I believe some of my tears were once again tied to Dawn.

"Now, don't you do that. You'll get me going again, too," Maggie's father replied, referring to my tears.

"I have so much respect for you," I repeated while still in an embrace.

I just didn't know what else to say. I wish I could have taken the pain away from him, but I knew that I couldn't. The meeting was short, and I ended it by asking him to relay a message of condolence to his wife. Maggie's father nodded and turned away. I was glad that I got the chance to speak with him.

The days following the death of the four students also brought me closer to an old friend again. Zach, the friend who rode on the bus with me from school, was now a junior at the high school and was experiencing firsthand how a school copes with losing friends and classmates.

During a phone conversation, we spoke of some of the similarities and differences between the tragedies of the accident and the suicides of Kevin and Dawn. Throughout the conversation, I could visualize the scene he was describing at the high school. It was very similar to the scene 4 years ago. Zach spoke about the kids being in shock, but the difference was that it was an accident.

When Kevin and Dawn committed suicide, it was by their own hands.

In the days following the crash, there was conversation and debate about how the crash happened, how senseless, and probably preventable it was. It was still an accident. In the case of Kevin and Dawn, there were no answers, only questions. It is difficult to make sense out of or rationalize a suicide.

I, along with others, had decided to attend Kevin Wolfe's funeral and graveside service. Even some of the players from Old Man's Gym came to pay their respects. I stood with Zach at the funeral and at the gravesite. Neither of us have ever specifically spoken of it, but both of us had found a new common ground, and our relationship was forever changed. We had shared together the loss of close friends and gained a new respect for one another. At the conclusion of the funeral service, we joined a motorcade and drove to the cemetery that sits on the campus of the local university. The line of cars seemed to go on forever. Students, family, and friends all converged at the cemetery.

Kevin's mother, father, sister, and brother walked to the gravesite first. Kevin's body was then carried from the hearse to the tent perched over his final resting spot. After his body was placed in position, all other mourners closed in around Kevin's family, who were seated next to the coffin.

The service itself didn't last long. There was a sense of finality as we heard the words "ashes to ashes and dust to dust." Soon after the priest finished the graveside service, the funeral director stated that the service was concluded and that everyone was free to return to their cars, but most continued to stand with family and friends. Those who did start to return to their cars did so in a very slow, deliberate manner. The reality began to set in, and there was an outpouring of emotion.

I began thinking about the different stages, the process of coping with grief that everyone experiences at one time or another.

(1) Shock. Regardless of the cause of death—suicide, accident, or old age—this is the normal human reaction, followed by

(2) An information-gathering time period which passes rapidly as details about who, what, where, why, and how become known, and our brain begins to work overtime in an attempt to make sense of the event.

(3) Then, after the initial shock has worn off and people start to process the loss, a numbness sets in and we find it difficult to imagine going on with life without the loved one. Only time and grieving with close family and friends helps us through this difficult time.

(4) Mourning. Attending a service, a wake, a celebration of life, visitation, funeral, or the gravesite itself can offer comfort to all who mourn with us. It's also a way we comfort ourselves. Make no mistake—services are not so much for the dead as they are for the living. Funeral services are a way for us to deal with what has happened and to find a way to move on.

(5) Reality. After the last service for the victim is over, reality sets in. We start to realize that we will never see the deceased again. We may even start to feel the numbness and emptiness again. The difference is that this feeling of numbness can last forever. It's the feeling of having a hole in one's heart. It's easy not to feel the full effect and reality of our loss during the funeral services because we are constantly surrounded by people that care for us and share our loss. The harsh reality hits us when we are expected to get back to our routine of living and the person that we have recently lost is no longer a part of our lives.

(6) Moving on. Trying to find a way to cope and move on is by far is the greatest challenge. There is no secret to getting over losing a loved one. Everybody handles it differently.

For some, the loss is so devastating that the thought of moving on feels like a betrayal to the one we have just lost. We lose sight of those around us who feel the same pain, and we forget how much we are needed by others who are still with us and love us. It's hard to move on and sometimes we fail to learn the valuable lesson that life goes on.

I believe time is our best ally. Losing a loved one can be one of the strongest and most painful emotions we will ever feel. I also have come to realize that losing a loved one to suicide is much worse. It is a pain that is difficult to let go of. We tend to believe that there was something more that we could have done. We do not understand why, and we cannot explain what is unexplainable.

After the service at the cemetery, we slowly made it back into our car and sat waiting for others who parked in front of us to return as well. Mourners walked at a turtle's pace, greeting and hugging others that were in their path as they made their way to their cars. Most just couldn't bring themselves to leave Kevin or each other. The cemetery was quiet except for the whimpers and cries of those leaving. Some university students with looks of curiosity on their faces were walking by on the other side of the fence, watching the people at the gravesite.

"Funerals are like car accidents. Everyone loves to gawk," I said.

No one in the car said anything. We just kept watching the scene before us.

Later that day, along with a few others, we decided to barbecue in Carl's garage and, naturally, the conversation centered on the accident and Kevin's funeral. It was one of the most profound discussions that I ever had with my group of friends. I think it's safe to say that typically when a bunch of guys get together, the conversation doesn't get real deep. However, this time it was different.

We began to talk about what happens when you die. One held the opinion that nothing happened when you die; others spoke of a glorious heaven; and still others spoke of hell. It was interesting to hear everyone's ideas about the next life, or the lack thereof. Carl unknowingly hit a nerve with me as the conversation progressed. He said he believed that those who commit an act such as suicide would go to hell. Carl and I had only been friends for a couple of years at the time, so he had no knowledge of my history concerning suicide. I said nothing in reply to his comments, but it brought Dawn's memory rushing back to me.

Dave, a high school friend who shared some of my history with Dawn and Kevin, quickly glanced in my direction. I gave him a quick look back and shook my head as if to say, "Don't bring it up." He didn't, and the conversation progressed past the topic of suicide.

The five of us never spoke of death again, but I will always remember that cookout as one of those rare, deep, male conversations. It was comforting for me to hear my friends talk about their feelings on this issue. It does our soul good to know that we are not alone and that we share some of the same fears, not only in death, but also in life. The accident of 1991 was another reminder of how fragile life can be. The tragedy has taught me that you don't have to be over the age of 80 to die. Death can come to our doorstep at any time.

I also have learned that we should not dwell upon death. Life is to be lived and celebrated. Not a minute of any day should be wasted. If you do not feel you are doing enough to achieve your goals, then change your strategy and approach to life. And if you have not made any goals, then make some. If you start to veer off your plan, then retool and find a way, but never give up. No matter how far you fall, you can get up and start again. You can do it!

Chapter 5

A Meeting by Chance

A few weeks after Kevin Wolfe's funeral, I went to Old Man's Gym to play basketball. While there, I began to think once again of Kevin. The gym carried too many memories of him not to. I thought about the last time I had been to the gym when Kevin had been there.

"He had no idea that it would be his last time here," I thought to myself. I began thinking that I could leave the gym that night and never return as well. My thoughts were running away from me, and I was obsessing about death. I know now that I was in the early stages of depression and struggling to find a way to move on. It wasn't so much that I was feeling lonely or empty from losing Kevin to a car accident, but it brought back the entire issue of death and memories of suicide. I thought maybe if I were to visit Kevin's grave, it might provide me with some clarity on the issue.

I drove out to the cemetery and parked my car. I had not been to the cemetery since Kevin's funeral, so I didn't know what kind of stone or marker to look for. I began to scan the cemetery in the area where I believed his grave to be. Without warning, I tripped on a gravestone. I put my arm down to brace my fall and looked at the stone that I had just stumbled over. As I read the name on the stone, I collapsed, sinking to the ground on my knees, and then I couldn't move at all.

Frozen, I stared at the name on the stone. I'm not sure how long I sat there on my knees, but it seemed like eternity. I felt my heart beat out of my chest, and my breathing become shallow. My entire body became ice-cold and numb. I just kept staring at the name on the stone that I had tripped over.

It was "Dawn"!

I was now face-to-face with the grave that I had sworn never to visit. I was in complete shock. I did not even know that she was buried at that cemetery. Since Dawn's death, I had always thought perhaps she was buried at a cemetery located north of town.

The last time I was this close to Dawn was on the bus ride home and then walking to her front door. It was as if I had gone back into time. I had never said good-bye to her since that day. I was supposed to see her again at the choir rehearsal that night, and now I found myself 4 years later on my knees in a cemetery, staring at her gravestone.

Remorse and guilt swept over me. I'm not exactly sure why, but I spoke out loud, first quietly and then louder. "I'm sorry, Dawn. I'm so sorry." The longer I sat there and said I was sorry, the more it became clear to me why I was sorry.

I was sorry for not being a better friend. I was sorry for not being able to see her pain. The truth is that I knew Dawn was sad and wasn't herself. I knew that she was struggling with finding her way and her place in life. And I was also sorry for not realizing that she was in her darkest place. I was sorry that I couldn't stop her from destroying herself.

There was more. All of a sudden, I was sorry for not being at her funeral and for not showing our friendship its proper respect. I was sorry that I had not come sooner to deliver peace and forgiveness, and not just for Dawn, but for both of us.

I knew Dawn very well. She would have wanted to apologize for all of the pain that she had caused. Her final answer to her problems, I'm sure, was not what she had expected. Dawn was a very loving and giving person. She would never have wanted to do permanent damage to the hearts of people she loved so dearly.

I was sorry I hadn't given us the opportunity to make peace. All I could do was pray that she understood my feelings and would forgive me. I never had so many emotions converge at once, and I never realized just how much I had missed Dawn until that moment.

There was so much I wanted to say and needed to say to Dawn. I told her how I wished that I had been smart enough to see her real pain on the bus ride home. I didn't understand what she had been talking about. In my attempt to make her feel better, I had only helped to remove her last barrier of doubt and helped to deliver her to a place that was dark and full of lies. I apologized for not being there when she needed me the most and for not being strong enough to help her through her problems. I had never before felt so shallow and helpless as I did that day at the cemetery.

After a while, I just sat on the grass and let my thoughts do the talking. My feelings for Dawn were still very real. I tried to imagine where she and I would be if she were alive. As for the problems that sent Dawn to the dark lie of suicide, none of them mattered anymore. It was all a waste—a waste to lose her and for her to lose her life.

I said out loud again, "Sorry, Dawn!" She should have been here in life with me. It wasn't my intention to yell, to ridicule, or to make her feel bad. I missed her and wished she were with me. I also wanted to let go of my anger. I no longer wanted to feel the way I had felt for the past 4 years, and I certainly did not want to carry the baggage around anymore. Whatever kind of friendship that I could have with Dawn, even if it were from the grave, I wanted. I wanted to honor her memory, finally, without honoring the decision she made.

I used our chance encounter that day to express my anger to Dawn, then to work through it, and finally to release it. I began to tell her about the days following her suicide. I explained how unfair I thought the conversation on the bus ride home was.

"How could you carry on one conversation and allow me to carry on with another?" I asked her.

I described the confusion and pain that she caused. Was she mad at us? How could she do this to us? Did she wish for us to suffer? I spoke louder at times than others. It was because of these unanswered questions that I could not attend her funeral and why I felt that I had to turn my back on her—because I refused to contribute attention to such a poor and selfish decision.

I also told her about Samantha. Telling Dawn about Samantha was hard, but I stayed true to my feelings and let her know that while I could not be sure that her suicide or Kevin's had anything to do with Samantha's actions, I believed that misery loves company, and perhaps one teenager's suicide provides comfort for others in that they are not alone in the decision.

"That's also why I couldn't go, Dawn," I said out loud. "I couldn't contribute to a bad decision."

I poured my heart out to Dawn that day at the cemetery. It was ironic that until that day, I hadn't even acknowledged her existence (because of my pent-up anger), but I suddenly had a lot to say. I probably spent the next 2 hours at Dawn's grave. I cried, yelled in anger, stared up in the sky, and I even laughed at some of the fond memories.

It was good to laugh and remember the good times. Until then, I only had shaken my head in despair when I thought of Dawn. I had never allowed myself to think about what had brought us close in the first place.

"You knew I was coming, didn't you?" I said to Dawn.

I couldn't help believing that our chance meeting wasn't so chancy after all. Dawn and I hadn't said goodbye since she walked into her house 4 years ago and killed herself.

I know what some of you are thinking. *This guy is wacky, right?* Well, maybe, but if you believe in that sort of thing, and I guess I do, you have to admit, it was one heck of a chance meeting.

I don't want anyone to misunderstand what I'm saying here either. I'm not suggesting that in death you somehow have control over people or events on this earth. I don't believe it works that way. I'm just saying that a coincidental encounter occurred, and it was a meeting that was long overdue and was very therapeutic.

Everything changed for me that day. I was angry then and remain angry today at Dawn's decision. There are times that I still shake my head and think to myself, "What a shame," but I don't carry the anger around with me any longer. I have forgiven Dawn because I know she would truly be sorry for her decision and for all of the pain she caused. I have to forgive her. She was my friend, and she has done enough time in my prison. It feels good to be able to remember Dawn and smile again. I now concentrate on the good times we shared and not just the tragedy of her suicide.

Since our meeting in '92, I have gone back to visit Dawn's gravesite. I still find it therapeutic, and it allows me to feel close to her again. Occasionally, I have brought flowers or some token from our past, a ritual more for the benefit of the living than for the dead.

Each time I visit, I share with her all of the developments in my life. I visited a few days before I got married, when my kids were born, when I bought my first home, and when I've changed jobs. I have told myself that by sharing these milestones with Dawn, she can, in a way, experience the events that she never got to experience on her own. I always try to imagine what she might say or how she might advise me about all of the events in my life. That's also when I start shaking my head again. She should be here to experience for herself all that life has to offer.

I suppose I'm not alone in talking to loved ones who have passed. While coaching a Little League baseball game one day, we needed one more run to win the game. It was the last inning, and we had a runner on third and two outs. The opposing coach called time out and went to the mound to talk to his pitcher.

I was coaching third base and decided to take the moment to walk toward left field. I remember looking up toward the sky and whispering to myself, "Hey, Dawn, if you're up there watching, you know, give me a hand here, huh?" I must have been down there a little longer than I thought because the next thing I heard was the crack of the bat and then the sound of 30 parents screaming.

I turned around and saw the ball land on the ground in front of the left fielder. The runner we had on third ran onto home plate to win the game. "You've got to be kidding me," I thought to myself as I ran toward home plate to join in the celebration. Since then, I have often thought of Dawn and have whispered a word or two to her when I have been in tight spots.

Again, I don't want to give the wrong impression. I don't really believe that Dawn had anything to do with winning baseball games or getting me out of any tight spots. And I certainly don't want to convey any false sense that someone you have lost is going to be able to fix games or help you win the lottery.

Nor do I have any insight into what happens to you when you die. I have my own beliefs on that subject, but that's all they are—my beliefs. I don't want to create any illusions that somehow you're automatically going to be sitting in some paradise, lounging around and playing god with the living back on earth. I can safely say that I don't believe in that. I only wish to convey that it comforts me to believe that Dawn is looking down on me from time to time.

The relationship that I have developed with Dawn since that day in the cemetery is what has given me strength to write this book. It is my feeling that Dawn would have wanted her life to mean something other than tragedy and inopportunity. So instead, I have used our story to help better educate and inform anyone who reads this book.

I want to stress the point that I'm honoring the memory of my friend Dawn and not her decision to end her life. All of the conversations that I have with her now are one-sided. I'm the only one talking. Dawn will never be back to share her true thoughts. I can only imagine them.

CHAPTER 6

What If?

What were they thinking? We have all asked that question about a suicide victim. My guess is that most that contemplate or commit suicide are immersed in a situation they cannot see an end to. They cannot conceive of a resolution to the problem. They feel hopeless, useless, and like a burden to others. They do not see a future that is absent of their current problems or state of mind. They see only the here and now.

Also, perhaps they feel shame. Our society has deemed certain behaviors or actions as failures. Filing for divorce or bankruptcy, losing a job, having a drug or gambling addiction, or suffering from a mental illness are all actions that we are made to feel ashamed of. We live in the real world, so we do care what people think, and we do care about how people view us. The difference, as I see it, between those who commit suicide and those who live to fight another day lies in the severity of the problem and the depth of the shame. Victims of suicide become convinced that their feelings of shame, guilt, failure, and pain will never go away. They feel that the odds are against them.

Also, they believe the lie that nobody understands what they are going through. I have news for them. They are wrong!

The fact of the matter is that the present problems that we face and encounter each day will most likely not be in our lives months or years from now. In addition, many of the people we associate ourselves with will most likely not be in our lives 20 years from now. There will, of course, be the familiar face that pops up from time to time, but for the most part, all of us move on with our lives. (That is why class reunions exist!) My guess is that in another 20 years, the people I surround myself with today will change yet again. That is life.

It is painfully obvious what happens to the people who are left behind after someone commits suicide, and had I chosen the same fate as my friends, I would have inflicted pain in the same way. However, I believe those who contemplate suicide are only thinking in the moment. They cannot see that they will be leaving behind people they have not even considered or have not even met. Have you ever thought of the people whom you would be leaving behind or people that you have never yet met? Have you ever wondered what might have been or what-if?

What I mean is, in the space of 20 years after the point where you thought of ending your life, your associations with people would have changed, your family would have grown, and your friends would have changed. Your future wife or husband would have married someone else, your kids would never have been born, and your friends would have to find someone else to golf or bowl with, and what about the 5-year-old kid that you saved when you were 27? What kid you ask. That is right. You never met him. You never met him because you committed suicide and because of that, the five year old drowned. Do you understand what I am talking about? Because you are not here anymore, others' lives are forever changed.

While you are caught up in the negative influence that you may think you have on others, you are not aware of the positive influence that you have on those currently around you and on those you have yet to meet. You are capable of doing great things for others. Think about this: instead of checking out, *don't* check out. Instead, dedicate your life to helping others. Do something positive. Move away if necessary, but make your life about something positive. What do you have to lose? You were planning to die anyway, right?

I actually wrote this chapter last and then plugged it into the middle of this book. I decided to write this chapter after a student whom I had asked to read the book asked me a question.

She asked me if I had ever thought of committing suicide. I hesitated to answer and tried to think of a way to avoid the entire question. I knew what the truth was, and even though I had been working on this project of suicide prevention, I did not want to tell her the truth because I was worried about what she might think of me. After all, at my high school, I had something of a rock star image, which, I admit, I enjoyed. If I were to tell the truth and tell her that I had thought about committing suicide once when I was younger, my image would be tarnished.

I asked her to repeat the question. I knew exactly what she had asked, but I was stalling, deciding whether to tell her the truth or to lie. When she asked the second time, I lied. I looked her straight in the eye and said, "Hell, no."

I lied. I was ashamed and hid from the truth. It has been bothering me ever since. I have been asking myself repeatedly how can I help others fight their demons if I cannot be honest about my own. So there it is. The truth is that I did contemplate suicide once. After the car accident in 1991, I fell into a deep depression and was consumed with thoughts of death. It was not until after stumbling onto Dawn's grave that I began to heal. I walked away from the edge of the cliff that I had come so close to.

I am not ashamed of my past. I believe all of us at some point have struggled with the weight of the world on us. Some of us struggle more than others. The difference is how close we have walked to the edge without jumping. Thankfully, I had the courage to seek help to begin my journey back from the brink, and I asked myself, "What-if?"

I want to do an exercise illustrating just what I am talking about, and I invite all of you to do the same at the end of this chapter. I think you will surprise yourself with just how important you are. Days following the student's question, I again asked myself, "What-if?" What would life be like had I not been here anymore? *"What-if?"* I think I have been clear about what life is like for those we leave behind. It is miserable. However, I was thinking about what life is like *now*, with me in it, and what life would be like now if I were *not* in it. What if you were suddenly gone and no longer alive? How would the lives of those close to you be affected? How would the world that you would have left behind be different? *That* is the exercise.

I will share with you some of the lives that I have had a positive impact on since that day I walked from the edge of the cliff, and I invite you to do the same in the exercise. It is important that you remain positive when you write how your life has affected others. This is not an exercise for negativity. Stay positive.

First example: Coaching Little League baseball

I remember the first time I gathered a group of 11- and 12-year-old boys together and explained how we were going to practice and play baseball. I was stunned by the look on their faces. They were hanging on every word. It was important to them that they not fail. I could see in their eyes that they did not want to disappoint me. They did not know it at the time, but that would have been impossible. They worked so hard and had so much pride in what they were doing that I could never have been disappointed. I viewed them as part of my family.

When I played Little League baseball, my coaches were like gods to me, and they instilled in me some of the values I hold today. I never wanted to disappoint them, either. I learned about teamwork, putting trust in others, and working through adversity. I would like to think that my young players thought of me in that same way.

It has been 20 years since I stepped to the edge of the cliff, and in that time, I have touched the lives of countless young players on the baseball field. Had I chosen to jump from the cliff, I would never have had the honor of being a part of their lives, and, I daresay, they would never have had the opportunity to have Coach Merrill in their lives. True, those boys would have played Little League baseball anyway, and yes, they still would have had a coach, but it would not have been me, and their experience would have been different. I am not saying that their experience would have been worse. I am saying, however, that the relationship that I had with those players was special. To this day, I stay in contact with most of them, and when they come home from college or elsewhere, they make a point to call or to buy their old coach a drink. You cannot buy that kind of friendship. I cherish those days. More of us should cherish the opportunity to have a positive impact on people's lives. I did. I did have a positive impact on their lives, and you have a positive impact on the lives that you touch every day, too.

Second example: My family

I almost become teary-eyed and upset when I think of depriving my two children, Andrew and Taylor, a chance to have life. Had I jumped from the cliff, they would not exist.

I did not know Lisa (my wife) at the time that I was in my darkest place at my darkest hour, but she would have gone on living and would have eventually met and married someone else, and would have had children, but they would not be Andrew and Taylor.

I cannot imagine that. I think of all that they have done so far in their young lives and the lives that they have already touched and had such a positive impact on. Sitting here writing this chapter, I can hear their laughter downstairs. I shake my head trying to imagine those sounds being replaced by silence. It would not be fair.

My son Andrew has autism and has an aide at school. Every night, his aide writes us of Andrew's progress and tells us what a delightful boy he is. I can almost see her smiling as she writes the message. He has had a positive impact on her life. Andrew plays baseball, soccer, basketball, flag football, takes guitar lessons, and is in Cub Scouts. He leaves something positive in every instance. Once again, none of that would have been possible if I had jumped from the edge.

My wife, Lisa, is a family physician. I need not mention how many years of hard work, study, and discipline are required for that profession. It demands commitment from the doctor as well as the spouse and family. Early in Lisa's career, she had considered pursuing a career that would not require as many hours away from home and her children. I would not allow it. I told her that she was destined to be a doctor and that she would some day save lives. I encouraged her to fulfill her dream of becoming a physician and gave her the support that is necessary in juggling a career and two children at the same time. Had I jumped instead of walking away, Lisa may not have become a doctor. She may never have had the opportunity to have a positive impact on her patients. The implications of that decision would have been life altering, for not only her, but also all of the lives she encounters every day.

Third example: My friends

Each year, a group of us goes out West for a week to play golf. It is the fastest 6 days of the year. The memories that we share and talk about the rest of the year are priceless. Wherever we may find ourselves, the stories of the golf trip at some point creep into the conversation and are told and retold in front of our wives and other friends. I mention this trip because its stories are ones that provide laughter and have positive effects for all of us.

All of us have someone that we would consider a best friend. If I include my high school years, I have been fortunate enough to have two of them. Your best friend is someone whom you would trust your life with and trust all of your secrets to. They are there when you are up, but more importantly, they are there when you are down. They never judge you, and they always defend you. You are never alone as long as you have them. It saddens me to think of their lives without me and my life without them. Again, none of what we have shared would have been possible had I jumped.

Do not get bogged down too much with having only one best friend. Open your mind and broaden your circle of confidants. Meet and be friendly to as many people as you can. Make a party of it, not just the two-man canoe, and for god's sake, do not let the little things in life and petty arguments get in the way of sharing memories that can last a lifetime.

Too many times, we are hit with tragedy that makes us remember what brought us close to our friends in the first place and only then do we realize what we have lost by allowing silly arguments to keep us apart. Keep your friends close. In the end, they are who we will need the most.

Fourth example: Others in my life

I have mentioned the people that I have surrounded myself with on an everyday basis—my baseball team, my family, and my friends. I have not mentioned, however, the hundreds, if not thousands, of people I meet every day, people that I may not know. I think of the woman at the bank that I held the door open for, the man who needed help getting his new table into the truck, the little boy who needed an extra 50 cents for his hot dog at the concession stand, or even the lost dog I returned to its owner.

We have opportunities to have a positive impact on thousands. Our lives are gifts and should be treated as such. Millions die each year from physical ailments, but these people fight. They do all that is necessary to live. We should not view mental illness any differently. We, too, should fight and do whatever is necessary to live. Our existence—our lives—are significant and important. We should not throw our lives away because of a problem that we confront. We are stronger than any demon, and we can defeat it.

Over the years, our friends and family may change, but we keep them in our hearts. At the same time, we constantly meet new people and forge new relationships. We start new careers, meet new people, and then meet the people in their lives. The dominos are endless, and so are our opportunities to make positive contributions in life.

Life is hard and painful. Good. It should be! I want it to be. It is the pain in life that makes us who and what we are. The obstacles that we face in life and how we choose to handle our adversities are how we learn and grow. We spend too much time thinking about the negative influences in life. I choose to think about the little things that make life great!

Our decisions in life have consequences. Our choices affect those around us and even those we have not yet met. We as individuals matter. It may never truly be possible for us to know just how many lives we touch throughout the course of our lives. I urge you to draw up a list of who means the most to you, and a list of the people you have impacted positively, including people you have yet to meet.

As I sit here staring at the computer screen, I have been thinking about just how different the world would be had I chosen to leave before my time. I can still hear the laughter downstairs. Thank God I did not jump!

CHAPTER 7

Tyler's Fight

Baseball is and has been a big part of my life. Of all the coaching positions that I have had, coaching Little League baseball has been my greatest joy. It puts a smile on my face anytime I think back on those days. It's fun to remember the games, teams, and all of the players from those summers, and I take the memories with me wherever I go. In 18 years of coaching baseball and basketball, I have coached at least 500 kids and student athletes, and I remember them all.

One child that I remember fondly was Tyler, a very talented baseball player on the city Little League. I mostly remember coaching against Tyler as he was generally on the opposing team. I was fortunate, however, to be part of a coaching staff that had Tyler on a travel baseball team.

Tyler was full of energy and emotion. He played a variety of positions on the field, which was not uncommon for a kid that age. Tyler played each position with the same vigor and aggressiveness to succeed and win—a trait that any coach loves to see in his players. Tyler was also something of a team clown. The only thing predictable about Tyler was that he was unpredictable.

Tyler was the second of three boys in his family. His younger brother, Dixon, and two of his cousins, Nick and Dean, were in the group I coached. By coaching all four of these boys, I also had the pleasure of becoming acquainted with their parents.

The Marten family was very involved in volunteering and working at the baseball park. Any time something was needed to be done, a member of this family would pitch in and help. Whether it was fixing a fence, putting up signs, writing a check, or managing the concession stand, the Martens were there. Anyone who came to the park knew someone in the Marten family.

Tyler's little brother, Dixon, was on one of the most successful Little League travel teams that Bowling Green had ever seen. I was and still am honored to have been the coach of that team. The Bowling Green Titus Realty baseball team (that was the team name) did a lot of traveling to many of the cities in Ohio as well as to Indiana, Michigan, and twice to the USSSA Little League World Series in Brainerd, Minnesota.

It was during these trips that I got to know Tyler's family the best, and it was also a time when Tyler began to suffer from depression, found himself in trouble at school, and began to withdraw from friends and the parts of life that gave him the most pleasure.

In an attempt to give Tyler a fresh start, his parents enrolled him in a private school out of state. It wasn't long, however, before Tyler found trouble at his new school and his depression worsened. He returned home, and he and his family then tried a variety of alternative schools, doctors, medications, social groups, and help groups. Wherever Tyler's family thought there could be assistance or a solution, they sought help in an attempt to bring back the Tyler that was fun loving and happy.

Tyler's parents, Gary and Deb, did everything they could to get their son back.

One sunny summer day as I was preparing for baseball practice, Tyler's mom, Deb, dropped off Dixon for practice at the ball field. She got out of the car and began walking toward me. She seemed happier than normal, with an extra bounce in her step.

"Hey, Deb, how are you doing?" I asked.

"Much better, I think," she replied, holding her fingers crossed.

"Why? What's up?" I answered curiously.

"Well, we got Tyler's medication turned around, and he seems to be showing improvement," she answered with a smile on her face.

Deb said that Tyler was feeling better, and he was making plans to improve in school. She went as far as to tell me that she had even seen Tyler make progress socially as well. He was around some of his old friends again and often brought his girlfriend by the house as well.

I was happy for their family. I prayed that Tyler's situation would continue to improve for his sake and his family's sake. The one thing worse than going through severe depression is watching someone close to you suffer from depression and not having the power to heal them. At the conclusion of our conversation, I watched Deb drive away. She was so happy, and I was happy for her, Tyler, and their whole family.

I heard the news about 6 months later. Tyler had committed suicide. He had lost his battle with mental illness and depression. Apparently, Tyler's demons got the best of him. One afternoon, he drove across the state line, and after mixing fertilizer with Mountain Dew, Tyler committed suicide by drinking it while sitting under a tree outside of a community hospital. I got sick to my stomach hearing of his demise.

I could only think of Tyler's parents and brothers. I knew all too well what was in store for them and Tyler's friends. I didn't want to believe the news. I wanted to remember the happier times, Tyler playing baseball at the Little League park, Tyler having fun with his friends in the dugout, Tyler eating Myles Pizza with sauce all over his face, Deb working in the concession stand taking care of all of the kids, and Tyler being happy. I could only shake my head at this tragedy.

What made Tyler's suicide so frustrating was that there was nothing more that his family could have done for him. They had tried everything that they could think of. They had gotten out the mental illness playbook and tried every play. They had tried the counselors, the medication, and all of the new starts and old starts for Tyler, and in the end, none of it worked. Imagine the frustration that Tyler's family must have felt and still feel. Tyler could not save himself from the dark demon of depression and suicide, and that is what makes his suicide so hard.

Tyler's funeral service took place at the church where he and his family had spent so many Sundays. His body was not present, but memories of Tyler were everywhere. There were pictures and mementos of Tyler's life. I, like most, strolled down memory lane in silence. As I looked at the pictures of Tyler, my mind was crowded. I found myself once again thinking of Harry, Kevin, and Dawn.

After my wife and I had taken our seats in the church, I scanned the room and saw many familiar faces. We could only imagine what Gary, Deb, and his brothers must have been feeling. They were living their worst nightmare imaginable. They had lost a son to suicide and to a disease that could not be stopped by all of the counselors, medications, fresh starts, and love they could provide.

Throughout the service, we heard stories of Tyler's life from his family, friends, and his girlfriend. I found myself staring into space. I couldn't snap out of it. There were too many similarities between Kevin's funeral and Tyler's. "Suicide," I thought to myself. "What is it in the human brain that triggers someone to commit such an act?"

Later that evening, I went to the Elks Club with some friends to have a drink and to try to divert our thoughts from Tyler's suicide. We were unsuccessful. No matter what we talked about, the conversation soon made its way back to Tyler. At some point, we just stopped trying to talk about anything else. We surrendered to what we were all feeling and began to exchange stories of Tyler.

For the better part of an hour, we shared our favorite memories of Tyler, mostly stories about him at the baseball park, about a play he made during a game, or about a joke he made after a game, but our conversations would always tail off at the end and slowly we'd shake our heads in reflection.

"What a shame." That was the phrase most commonly repeated that night.

No one wanted to believe Tyler was gone or that he had committed suicide. At the end of the night, Cary, a close friend of mine, raised his glass and gave a toast to Tyler and to better times. I raised my glass and then interrupted the toast.

"Let's drink to better times, but let's also drink to Deb and Gary," I said.

My comments evoked a longer silence from my friends, but that silence was broken by Cary raising his glass even higher and then saying, "To Gary and Deb."

I felt my toast was more appropriate. Gary and Deb had done what any good parents would have done. They had done everything they could think of to help Tyler, they had exhausted every resource available to them, they had sought out every medical regimen, and in the end, they probably believed the lie that they had failed. The truth is that they didn't fail. They didn't fail because they never gave up fighting the demon. Tyler did.

That's what the demon of depression and suicide does. It allows victims to believe that there is no hope or way out. It makes people feel alone and does not allow the victims to feel the power of the love being offered by those closest to them. The demon of suicide is powerful and affects not only the victims but the ones closest to them as well. The demon seduces survivors into thinking that they are flawed and inadequate.

Unfortunately for Deb and Gary, the worst was yet to come. They would have to find a new path of existence. They would have to find a life that did not include Tyler. That path is difficult and sometimes those closest to a victim of suicide are unable to find it, so my toast went to Tyler's parents, family, and friends, and I prayed that they would all find their way and would be able to move forward.

It wasn't that I didn't want to drink to Tyler, but his suicide made me sad and angry. Once again, someone close to us had chosen to stop fighting the demon and leave us behind. The demon is powerful, and I sympathize with those who battle and tire from the fight, but we must never give up.

Now when I hear of someone losing his or her battle against depression and committing suicide, I become enraged. I visualize the demon laughing at us and basking in yet another victory. My advice to that demon is, "Keep laughing. Your days are numbered. I plan to fight and help others fight you for years to come."

Weeks and months after Tyler's suicide, I learned from others that Tyler believed he had been a burden on his parents who had dealt with his never-ending sadness, up-and-down mood swings, and depression. Committing suicide, though, only intensifies the burden on the family.

Losing loved ones to their battle against depression is much more painful than helping them continue their fight. Suicide victims often do not understand this fact and for some reason, probably believe in a fantasy that we will all simply pick up the pieces and will go on to live wonderful and happier lives without them.

I wish that victims of suicide like Tyler had had the opportunity to talk to my friends Harry, Kevin, Dawn, or had talked to Samantha, who attempted to take her own life. They would have told Tyler that suicide was not the answer.

CHAPTER 8

Derek

The spring of 2004 was my second year as head baseball coach at Bowling Green High School. After school that day, the varsity baseball team practice schedule called for batting practice indoors, followed by field practice outside starting at 4:00.

The practice had been as usual, however, that all changed between 4:00 and 4:30. The team had stopped in the locker room to change and prepare for practice outside, and I was sitting in the coaches' office when Aaron, my assistant coach, walked in the office and received my attention.

"I think we have a problem here, Coach," Aaron said.

"What's the problem?" I asked.

"There's a rumor out here that Derek killed himself."

"What?" I asked.

I sat up from my slouched position and tried to process what Aaron had just told me. I had clearly heard what Aaron had said but was in shock at the same time. Derek was a sophomore in high school and a member of the junior varsity baseball team. Derek should have been on the practice field, so how could he have committed suicide, I thought.

"The kids are saying that Derek killed himself," Aaron repeated, answering my question.

I rose from my chair and proceeded to walk past him and into the locker room. I didn't get far when I spotted Moe, a track runner, sitting in the corner of the locker room with his hands over his face and sobbing. I knew at that moment that the rumor was not a hoax. Moe would not be sobbing because of a rumor. I went to him and asked what was wrong. I was still hoping the rumor was just an exaggeration.

"Moe, what's wrong?"

"Derek . . . man, he's dead," Moe answered.

I sat down next to him trying to stay calm but also trying to understand what he was saying.

"What happened?" I asked in a shocked panic.

"Coach threw him out of practice, and he went home and killed himself," Moe said hysterically.

I began to put my arm around Moe, but he quickly shook me off.

"No, man . . . get off me. Fucking coach," Moe said, pulling away and still sobbing over the shock of hearing that he had just lost a friend.

Just then, a few other baseball players had entered the locker room.

"Coach, Derek killed himself," one of the guys yelled out.

"I know, guys, try to take it easy," I replied.

Just as I spoke, Moe stood up and tried to leave the locker room.

"Moe, where are you going?" I asked.

"Getting the fuck out of here," Moe insisted.

I attempted several times to calm him down and finally succeeded in making him stay in the locker room.

I was unsure of his mental state and was not about to allow him to leave unsupervised. The last thing I needed was for Moe to leave the school and do something stupid by hurting himself or getting in a car and possibly hurting someone else.

A few minutes later, I walked outside and peered out toward the baseball complex located about 500 yards to the north of the school. I was hoping to learn something, anything. A few other kids who were coming in slowly from the track and the softball/baseball complex met me. They were all moving like zombies. I could tell that all of them had already somehow heard of Derek's fate.

I turned to walk back into the school when I noticed Moe behind me.

"Coach, I'm going out to the baseball field," Moe said.

"Wait, I'll drive out. Let's go," I replied.

We jumped in my truck and started out. My mind was racing, and I had the chills from head to toe.

"Moe, you said that Derek had been sent home from practice?" I asked.

"I went back into the locker room to get something for track, and Derek was in there getting his stuff. He told me that he got kicked out of baseball practice for having tobacco in his mouth and then just said he was out of here."

Moe paused for a moment and then continued. "I tried to tell him not to worry about it, but he just kept going."

Moe was much calmer now. I still didn't have any answers to the what, why, how, and when questions, but I was hoping to gain that information out at the field.

We got out of the truck and started toward the field. We saw about 10 to 15 girls that were on the softball team and roughly the same number of junior varsity baseball players. The girls were sitting on the ground next to the batting cage. All were very emotional and doing their best to keep themselves together. Most of the boys were sitting or leaning on the bleachers and staring into space.

Greg, our head softball coach, was still at the complex and talking with his assistant coaches about what I'm sure was Derek's suicide. After a quick nod to Greg, a couple of J.V. baseball players approached and met me with an embrace. Obviously, they were very emotional as was everyone upon hearing the news of Derek's suicide.

Surveying the scene at the complex, I noticed Becky, a softball player whom I had known for a long time. In fact, years ago, I had coached her in baseball. She was sitting on the ground with her friends. I knew both of her parents and knew that they were out of town. Being a father myself, I thought her parents should know what had happened and would want to talk with their daughter. I went behind the dugout and called them on my cell phone. I began to tell them about Derek, but they had already heard the news. News does travel fast, I thought.

I told them that I was at the softball/baseball complex, as was Becky, and they immediately asked to speak to her. While she was using the phone, I spotted Josh, the junior varsity baseball coach, sitting on the opposite bleachers by himself and went over to see how he was doing. He was white as a ghost—clearly, still in shock. I stood next to him for a few minutes.

"What happened, Josh?"

Josh continued his silence for an additional minute, then whispered, "I sent him home." He answered while still gazing at the empty baseball field.

I looked over my shoulder toward the front gate of the complex and could see Jeff Dever, our high school principal, Mr. Caumartin, our superintendent, and a sheriff's deputy walking toward us. Instead of pressing Josh with any more questions or asking him to explain why he sent Derek home, I waited for the three men to arrive.

There was no point in having Josh repeat himself once they arrived.

Most of the kids just watched in silence as the three men walked past them and made their way toward Josh and me.

"How you guys doing?" Mr. Dever asked.

Josh remained quiet and resumed his posture of sitting and staring at the empty field.

"Okay," I said, answering Mr. Dever's question.

Mr. Dever introduced the sheriff's deputy and said that the deputy had a couple of questions. While both Mr. Dever and Mr. Caumartin spoke with Josh by the bleachers, I walked behind the dugout to speak with the deputy.

He began by asking what I knew about the incident and what my perspective was on the situation. I informed him that I was the varsity coach and that we were inside the building while the junior varsity team was out on the field practicing. I had only heard of the tragedy from others that were coming into the building.

I asked him if Derek was indeed dead and if he had truly taken his own life. I know it might sound like a stupid question, but I wanted to hear it from a sheriff's deputy and not only our students. The deputy nodded his head quickly and confirmed that Derek was indeed dead and had committed suicide.

I remembered both Moe and Josh had mentioned that Derek was sent home from practice.

"What time did you or 911 receive the call?" I asked.

"I was called around 3:25 and arrived at the victim's home around 3:30," the deputy responded.

"Was he already gone?" I continued.

The deputy nodded, indicating that Derek had already died by the time he had arrived.

Neither of us spoke for a moment as I attempted to process all of the information. The deputy broke the silence by asking questions such as, what kind of kid was Derek, had I known Derek to have any drug problems, had I noticed Derek going through any type of depression, and had I heard Derek talk about wanting to end his life.

I answered no to his last three questions. Derek was a good kid who had many friends and was a fairly good baseball player. I had never heard of Derek having trouble with his grades or being a discipline problem in school. Derek's suicide was as much a shock to me as it was to anyone else.

At the conclusion of our talk, the deputy and I walked back toward the bleachers where Josh was talking with Mr. Dever and Mr. Caumartin. I could tell that Josh was describing the events after school that led to Derek's suicide.

"I'm sorry, were you talking about what happened after school?" the deputy asked, turning his attention to Josh.

Josh nodded.

"Could you tell me what happened when you all came out to practice?" the deputy inquired.

"The kids had stretched their arms and started long tossing (playing catch, starting close, and then extending their distance) when I noticed a bulge in Derek's mouth. As I came closer, I could tell that it was, in fact, tobacco."

"What happened next?" the deputy pressed.

"I couldn't believe that he had it in his mouth," Josh explained to the four of us.

"Did you tell him that tobacco was against the rules of the team and the school?" Mr. Caumartin asked.

"Yes, I told him that he couldn't have tobacco. He knew he wasn't allowed to have it. That's why I couldn't believe he had it in his mouth—and so blatantly! He wasn't even trying to hide it," Josh explained.

"Then what happened?" the deputy continued.

"I asked him why he was being so stupid having the tobacco in his mouth. He knew that Coach Merrill had just dismissed a varsity player last weekend for other disciplinary reasons (Josh was referring to a varsity player that had been expelled from the team).

"He just stared at me and didn't say anything. I didn't tell him to go home. I just told him he couldn't be at practice, and he would have to talk to Coach Merrill and see what, if any, punishment there would be tomorrow," Josh continued.

"And then he left?" asked the deputy.

"Yep, and we continued with practice."

"What time do you think that might have been?" the deputy asked.

"Probably about 3:00," Josh answered.

I mentally began to put a timeline together. School ends at 2:30. Derek, along with other players, hurried to the locker room, changed their clothes, and headed out to the baseball field. After being dismissed/ejected from baseball practice, Derek stopped in the locker room and spoke with Moe. It must have been at least 3:05 to 3:10 by then.

From school, Derek would have taken the 5-minute drive to his home just outside of town, and would have arrived at home at around 3:10 to 3:15. The deputy told me that he received a call to go out to Derek's house at or around 3:25 to 3:30. That means that Derek would have had no more than 10 to 15 minutes to plan, prepare, and finally to implement his plan of self-destruction.

The conversation lasted for another 10 to 20 minutes before the sheriff's deputy had enough information, or at least as much as he was going to collect from us, and left. After receiving a phone call, Mr. Dever and Mr. Caumartin left as well. Josh and I remained at the field and discussed Derek's suicide for a while longer.

Josh was still in shock and motionless. The look on his face was very familiar to me.

"Are you going to be okay?" I asked.

"Yeah, I'm just going to go home," he muttered.

"I'll call you tonight and see how you're doing. Okay?"

"Thanks, Coach," Josh replied climbing into his car.

I returned to the school and walked to the office to see if there was any further information about Derek's suicide. Upon arriving in the main office, I could see Mr. Dever, Mrs. Tache, our assistant principal, Mr. Vannett, our athletic director, a few counselors, and a man who looked familiar, but whom I could not place. I sat down in a chair across from Mr. Dever's desk and simply listened to their conversation.

The meeting lasted for nearly an hour. The group discussed the various details of the tragedy, but the focus was on how best to provide support for our students.

While listening to the conversation, I wondered if this meeting was similar to the ones held when Kevin and Dawn died, and when Samantha attempted suicide, and when the car accident of '91 claimed four students' lives.

A few people in the office began speculating on where Derek's funeral would be and how many people would be attending.

"Why don't you call the family and offer to have the funeral in the gymnasium to accommodate the number of people?" a counselor said, turning her attention to our principal.

"No, you can't do that!" I blurted out.

The room got quiet and some heads snapped over to look at me. At first, I thought, "Oh, crap, I probably overstepped my bounds." However, a second later, I didn't care. Having Derek's funeral in the gymnasium was a terrible idea.

"This is exactly what we did wrong 15 years ago. You don't want to glamorize a suicide," I explained.

Just as the counselor began to address my concerns, Mrs. Tache, our vice principal, who was also a teacher in the Bowling Green system 17 years ago, interrupted and added, "I agree with Doug."

For the next 5 minutes, she went on to explain to everyone still in the room that this was not the first time our school had been through the tragedy of suicide. I chimed in periodically throughout her explanation, filling in the blanks and giving my opinion about the mistakes we made and why we should not repeat them.

With the discussion coming to a close, I decided to leave. I had heard that some of Derek's teammates and friends had gathered at the home of Derek's cousin and teammate. I decided to drive over to check on them and see if I could help in any way. As I started down the hallway toward the exit, Mr. Dever yelled to me, getting my attention.

"Doug."

He was walking toward me with the man whom I recognized but could not place.

"Doug, I want you to meet Bill Donnelly from CRC."

"Bill?" I said.

"How are you, Doug?" Bill replied.

It hit me almost like a ton of bricks. Bill was the counselor from Children's Resource Center (CRC) who had talked to me 17 years ago. Things had really come full circle for me now. Instantly, I was reminded of those times when I struggled with the suicides of Harry, Kevin, Dawn, Samantha, and Tyler.

"We've met," Bill commented to Mr. Dever.

Just after he said that, Mr. Dever was called back into the office to take a phone call.

"Did you know it was me?" I asked Bill.

"I did. Mr. Dever mentioned your name as the baseball coach, and when I saw you walk in, I knew it was you."

I didn't really know what to say next. It was good to see Bill again; on the other hand, I only wish it had been under better circumstances. I knew that our students would benefit from his presence and his experience in dealing with the tragedy of teenage suicide.

"You were right about not wanting Derek's funeral in the gymnasium," Bill assured me.

"I am just worried that we will make the same mistakes and glamorize Derek's decision to commit suicide," I began to explain.

"I know, I know. I agree," Bill added.

Unfortunately, our conversation was brief and ended there when he was called back into the office. Before he left, however, he mentioned that he would like to find time to talk tomorrow. I was beginning to realize the magnitude of what everyone would be going through in the coming days and weeks, and for some, in the months and years ahead.

I must confess that I was a little nervous going to the house where everyone was. I was unsure how I would be received. I began to think about Josh and how he had sent Derek home. I also thought of Moe's first reaction upon hearing the news of Derek's suicide. He had blamed Josh and me for sending Derek home.

I prayed that no one else felt the same way. I hoped that everyone would have had enough time to realize what I already knew—Derek's suicide was not anyone's fault. It was Derek's decision, and Josh was only a pawn in Derek's plan.

Without proper directions, finding the right house proved a little more difficult than I thought it would be. There were cars lined up on both sides of the street the distance of about 15 houses. I was able to find the right home, though, by observing several kids in the front yard of one of the houses. I parked down the street and began to walk up the sidewalk. I was still nervous as I walked to the house, but I knew that it was the right thing to do.

I was greeted by Derek's uncle Kevin in the driveway. He extended his hand and gave me a warm welcome.

"Hi, Doug, glad you could come. Everyone is inside and would love to see you."

It was like taking a piano off my back to be received so warmly. After exchanging greetings and small talk, I went in and proceeded into the main living area where most of the kids were sitting and talking. The scene was very reminiscent of the aftermath of Kevin's suicide. Jesse, one of our baseball players, greeted me first.

He immediately stood up, arms outstretched, and gave me a long hug. He would never know it, but Jesse gave me just the icebreaker I needed. From there, I made my way around the room giving condolences to everyone I knew.

I didn't want to spend too much time with the kids in the living room. I knew that kids behave differently in the company of adults and coaches, and I wanted to give them space and time to be themselves, so I moved into the kitchen where many of the parents and family friends were. I was again greeted very warmly and actually with great appreciation. I joined most of them for refreshments and conversation. Many of them asked what was going on at the high school, but most of them asked if I had had a chance to talk with Josh and wondered how he was doing. The outpouring of concern and support was overwhelming.

I knew that Josh had gone home to his parents' house and was probably not only grieving the loss of a player, but replaying the day's events in his mind over and over again, wondering what he could have done differently. I knew exactly how he felt.

I felt such support from the parents that I thought I should share some of that support with Josh. I mentioned to the parents that I was planning to visit Josh before going home. They asked me to convey their support and to extend their invitation for him to come over and join them. I said I would and again thanked them for all of their support.

Josh was still very much shaken by the entire ordeal. I passed on the message of support from the parents and extended their invitation for him to join them. Josh seemed at little more at ease with the news of their support, although he was still visibly very distraught.

"I'm still not ready to see that many people. I just don't know what to say."

I understood. I didn't want to talk with anyone either after Dawn had committed suicide. I think you simply go through a period where you have to try and make sense out of it yourself before you can share with other people. The problem is that you're never going to make any sense out of something that doesn't make any sense.

The next day I arrived at school early. I knew it was going to be a hard day for everyone. It was a familiar scene in the halls. Many of the students were crying, hugging, and doing their best to deal with the shock of Derek's death. Counselors could also be seen around almost every corner, and teachers were doing their best to provide understanding and support. It was a complete flashback to 1987 for me. The faces were different, but everything else was the exact same. I proceeded toward the office to see if I could gather any information concerning the day ahead of us.

"Come on in, Doug," Mr. Dever yelled out to me.

I went in and again took a seat across from Mr. Dever's desk.

"How you doing, man?" he asked.

Mr. Dever always has a way of making you feel good, even though you might not be. He has the gift of handling crises in a way that is both sympathetic and strong. He exudes confidence and gives people strength.

"I'm okay, Boss," I responded.

"I'm glad you're here. You do a great job with these kids."

I felt at ease and as if I belonged to part of a larger team in dealing with the tragedy upon us. I listened to the conversation intently and made suggestions as different concerns were raised.

During the meeting, I learned that a church service was scheduled for later that evening and would be officiated by one of the reverends that had been present since the news of the tragedy. I focused on attempting to prevent any decisions that might give the appearance of glamorizing Derek's suicide. My message was simple. Honor the person but not the decision.

We were particularly concerned about Derek's teammates. Both the varsity and junior varsity team were close to Derek and were having a hard time dealing with how he died—not only that he had decided to end his life, but also that Derek had spent all day with them yesterday in school and then for a short period of time at practice.

I can certainly understand how difficult it can be to spend the last moments with someone before their death. Josh was not alone in wondering what he could have done differently to prevent Derek's suicide. Many of the kids were wondering the same thing. It's probably normal to feel that way. We relive the last moments spent with the victim and wonder if we missed any signs. We don't always find what we're looking for, but we still feel guilty for not being able to stop the victim's self-destruction. In fact, very seldom are there any real signs of the victim's suicide plans.

The counselors suggested that I speak with the team about the tragedy. An announcement was made on the public address system and shortly after 10:00, all baseball players went to the auxiliary gym for a meeting. Their parents were invited to join, as well. To my surprise, at least half of the players' parents attended the meeting.

Bill joined me as I made my way down to the gym. I asked him many questions and wanted to make sure that I sent the right message. We prepared for approximately 10 minutes as he helped me form my message and sort my thoughts and feelings. Just before I walked in to the gym where the players and parents sat patiently waiting, I peeked in the door to get an idea of what I was walking into. The bleachers were full of parents, students, counselors, teachers, and administrators. It was a full house. This will not be easy, I thought. Bill sensed my anxiety and put his hand on my shoulder.

"You'll be fine. I'll be right here by the door."

Bill and I came up with a couple of nonverbal cues so I wouldn't forget anything that I planned to say. I walked into the gym where my audience was waiting.

Then I centered myself in front of the group and took a deep breath. The room began to grow quiet with my presence. I scanned the room to grasp the full scope of who was in attendance. Aside from a few counselors that I had not met (from CRC, I assumed), I knew everyone there. I was still amazed at how many parents had come to be with their sons.

I began by expressing sorrow for the circumstances of our meeting. I then began my message, and my message was simple. SHARE. Share what is on your mind. Share with your parents, friends, teachers, counselors, or whomever you trust, but share. And not just a little bit. Share it all. Don't be tough or think that it is not cool to be in pain, and don't think that you're alone with your feelings. The truth is that all of us, at times, are in pain and feel sad.

I told them I fully understood their pain of losing a friend to suicide. I let them know that it is okay to have the emotions they have. Feelings of confusion, sadness, weakness, and anger are all normal, acceptable feelings. Anger is especially understandable. Derek chose to leave us, and while we can miss him, remember him, and hurt for him, we should not honor his decision. Instead, we should focus on what he meant to us and why we called him our friend in the first place.

"The next few days will be hard. I understand that there is a service tonight. Undoubtedly, there will be a visitation the next day followed by a funeral service. It is important that we stay together, share our feelings, remember what we loved about Derek, but most of all, we must remember what a shame it is that Derek will not be with us to experience any of the wonderful things that life has to offer. Suicide is not a viable option to our problems and should not be viewed as a solution or a new beginning. Suicide is an end," I voiced with a certainty.

I ended by asking the junior varsity and the varsity teams to meet in separate groups with their parents to discuss what course of action, if any, should be taken in the next couple of days to alter our baseball schedule in any way. I wanted to leave this decision primarily up to the kids but certainly wanted to involve the parents as well. I had been coaching long enough to know that you can't force kids to do something that is not in their hearts, especially to expect them to play a game a few days after a teammate's death. I also wanted the parents to be on the ground floor of that decision, should there be any concern over it.

Before I had a chance to join the varsity team at the top corner of the bleachers, several parents had approached to offer their support and to state their appreciation for sharing and speaking with their kids. Again, I was relieved to receive such support from our players' parents. It meant a lot to me.

As one parent approached to give me a hug, I broke down. I'm sure she was not expecting it, but she was very warm and supportive. She held me closer as I cried. I'm sure everyone in the gym noticed, and I was at first embarrassed. I couldn't help it. No one was more surprised by my tears than I was. I suppose I was simply overwhelmed by the cumulative effects of Derek's suicide, the stress it placed on the players, and memories of Kevin and Dawn.

I took the varsity team up to the top of the bleachers and asked them how they wanted to handle the schedule and the services that were to follow. My personal feeling on the subject was to play. I didn't want to send the message of giving more attention to a bad decision. I also thought it would be better for the kids to follow a normal schedule as close as possible. The next couple of days would be hard enough. To my surprise, it was unanimous, without any debate or conversation. Every player had decided to play the next scheduled game. A couple of them said they wanted to get back to the field as quickly as possible to give them a break from dealing with Derek's suicide.

I understood how they felt. The baseball field provided them with a release and a mental break from having to deal with the tragedy. I was equally and pleasantly surprised to know that the junior varsity team had made the same decision as well.

I stayed at the school for the remainder of the day and made myself available to all of the students. I had a connection with them and wanted to help in any way I could. I planned to help simply by listening.

Around lunchtime, Jesse, the student baseball player who greeted me the night before, approached to talk about how everyone has been dealing with the tragedy. Even as Jesse approached, I could tell that he had been crying and was still visibly upset. I pulled him aside in the hallway and gave him time to speak his mind. Through the course of the discussion, he mentioned that a shrine had been made at Derek's locker and asked if I would walk with him to the locker. As we reached that area, I could see two or three students standing in front of the locker holding each other. There were flowers, letters, pictures, and memorabilia from Derek's life sitting in front of and hanging off the locker. I didn't let Jesse see my disapproval of the shrine. I had flashbacks to the day after Kevin and Dawn ended their lives, and I remembered the shrines at the lockers and the flag at half-mast as well. It's not that I don't understand why we do these things, it's just that I believe we run the risk of sending the wrong message.

Those who have seriously or even casually considered committing suicide may see the act as a way to gain attention or popularity. What they fail to understand is that time marches forward, people recover, your suicide becomes a remember-when story—and you're still dead! That type of popularity never lasts.

Standing in front of Derek's locker, I looked over some of the material a little closer. There were letters, pictures, and mementos of Derek's past, but some of what I saw gave me pause and concern. I read one of the letters that spoke of Derek in heaven. Jesse was reading the letter over my shoulder when he asked me if I thought Derek was in heaven.

I freaked out a little. *The bus ride home*, I thought. I was not prepared for Jesse's question. I tried hard not to let him see my discomfort with the question, yet Jesse sensed something wrong.

"Are you okay, Coach?"

"Yeah, Jesse, it's just that your question reminded me of an old friend of mine."

Jesse was still looking at me and waiting for an answer to his question when out of nowhere the answer came to me.

"I don't know, Jesse. I don't know what happens when people die, and I don't know what happens when people commit suicide. I have my own opinions on what happens when we die, but that's all they are, my opinions."

That was it! That was the answer to Dawn's question, and it was the answer that came to me in front of Derek's locker. Jesse had scared me to death with his question, and why shouldn't I have been scared? The last time I had been asked that question, Dawn went inside her house and hanged herself. I was scared to death I might say the wrong thing, and Jesse would wind up with a rope around his neck. "No way," I said to myself, "not this time."

As soon as my conversation was over, I alerted our administration and counselors that I was concerned about Jesse. I was relieved to hear that the counselors and his parents were already aware of Jesse's grief and were dealing with it.

Later that evening, along with several students, I attended the church service that was designed to help students cope with Derek's suicide. After exchanging pleasantries with clergy, parents, and students, I took my seat at the back of the church. I watched the service with a great deal of curiosity and paid extra attention to the clergy and the tone that they set as dealing with the suicide. I was happy to see that, for the most part, Derek's death was not being glamorized.

At one point during the service, the minister invited Derek's friends to come forward and write sentiments about Derek on an overhead projector. The messages were very similar to the ones on Derek's locker—about loving Derek and missing him.

Afterwards, I wondered if the service had helped the healing process or if it had promoted the popularity of a bad decision. I kept comparing the last day and a half with the days that followed Kevin's suicide.

In the days following, I made an effort to talk with Josh, who was struggling over Derek's suicide. Josh was the one who had sent Derek out of practice for having tobacco in his mouth. Josh, I'm sure, was agonizing about whether or not he made the right decision about sending Derek out of practice. He felt responsible for Derek's death, just as I had felt responsible for Dawn's death. I reassured Josh that he was not to blame for Derek's suicide. I reminded him of the timeline. Derek would not have had time to drive home, go into the garage, set up his plan, and then execute that plan in less than 30 minutes. It was my opinion that Derek would not have had time to accomplish all of these things in 30 minutes if he hadn't already at least thought of committing suicide previously.

Through most of our discussion, Josh continued to listen, but I never really thought I was getting through to him. And at one point, Josh said, shaking his head, "You just don't understand."

"You're wrong," I said.

"How?" he replied.

I paused for a moment, reminding myself that I had said I would never speak of Dawn's or Kevin's suicides again. I took a deep breath and looked at Josh, who was still waiting for an answer to his question.

"Because when I was kid in high school here, I lost two of my best friends, both to suicide."

Josh's face changed from ashen, self-absorbed grief to one of surprise and interest.

"And when Dawn died, I was the last to talk with her. Our entire ride home on the bus was about the other friend that we had both just lost the week before. She was talking about one thing, and I was talking about another," I continued.

For the next 20 minutes, I found myself reliving the pain of both Kevin's and Dawn's suicides. Afterwards, I thought to myself how ironic it was that I had vowed never to talk about those tragedies again, and here I was, pouring out their stories 15 years later to someone in a similar situation.

After hearing my story, Josh's demeanor became receptive and he began to talk about Derek's suicide. I knew what he was feeling. He wished he could have done more to help. We all did.

At the conclusion of our discussion, I walked down to the coaches' office to grab a couple of things and then went out to my car to head home for a while. Driving out of the parking lot, my cell phone rang. It was Josh.

"Are you still here at the school?" he asked.

"Just about to leave the parking lot," I answered.

"Do me a favor and circle back around. I want to talk to you."

"Is it important?" I asked, wanting to get home even if it were only for a little bit.

"Yeah, sorry, but I just need to see you again real quick," Josh insisted.

"Okay, I'll be right there. Meet me in front of the band room door," I requested.

I pulled up to the door as I said I would, and I could see Josh standing on the sidewalk talking to a woman. The woman looked somewhat familiar. I figured it was either a counselor or a parent of one the baseball players that I had yet to meet. Instead of getting out of the car, I lowered the window to see what the emergency was. Josh and the woman walked closer to the car, and Josh began to introduce us.

"Hey, Doug, this is Gail. She would like to talk with you a little bit," Josh stated.

The look on my face had to be one of complete shock and surprise. The familiar face was no longer just a familiar one. Gail was Dawn's stepmother. Gail was one of the last people that I expected to see that day. I hadn't spoken with her since I was a kid calling the house to talk with Dawn. It had been 15 years since Dawn's suicide.

I hadn't wanted to talk to anyone after Dawn's suicide—not counselors, not teachers, not friends, not her family, nor even my own family. I was so angry that I just wanted Dawn's suicide to go away. I pretended that I hadn't even known her, that she never even existed. I knew now, however, as I sat in my car and watched Gail cross the street and move to the passenger side of the car, that all of that was about to change. I was about to have the conversation that I had avoided. Avoided for 15 years.

When Gail sat down and began to talk, I didn't hear a word she said. I was still numb from the shock of her being there. It was hard for me to grasp that after 15 years of silence and no communication with any of Dawn's parents, that an unexpected phone call from Josh would force this inevitable meeting. The closest I had ever come to talking with any of Dawn's family since her suicide was with her brother, Brett.

Brett was young when Dawn died, and I never knew for sure if he had remembered me in relation to his older sister. In my earlier years of coaching Little League, I coached on a team that rivaled Brett's. I eventually had the opportunity to coach Brett one summer on an all-star team. I never indicated to him that I knew his sister, but one day as I was giving him a ride home, he started to get out of the car and stopped. He turned back into the car and asked,

"You knew my sister, didn't you?"

I was startled by the question and by how direct Brett was in asking it.

"Yes, Brett, I did."

He climbed back into the car, and we talked about the times that he remembered about Dawn and what he knew of her and me. He was younger then, so some of his memories of Dawn were a bit vague, but it was good to hear the stories anyway. For that one afternoon, she was alive to me again. It was nice. I knew she was gone, though, and that she wasn't coming back.

I had always remembered Dawn's father, Keith, who was a homebuilder and an inspector. Since I had spent some time selling real estate and had always kept my license, I sent referrals to Keith any time the opportunity arose. Keith probably figured that I gave him referrals because of our acquaintance from the Little League park or something, but I always did it for Dawn. I guess I thought she would have liked that.

Other than my encounter with Brett and the referrals to Dawn's father, I had not had any contact with her family. I suppose I avoided having a conversation with them out of fear that it would simply be too painful for all of us. In the back of my mind, I always thought that some day I would eventually have a conversation about Dawn with one or all of her parents, but I certainly never anticipated it was going to happen after the suicide of another high school student.

Once Gail sat down next to me in the front seat of the car, I found myself staring at her. Memories of Dawn came rushing at me like a linebacker rushing the quarterback. I just kept staring at her. She reminded me so much of Dawn that I had to apologize for my staring.

"I'm sorry, you just remind me so much of Dawn," I started.

"Well, thank you, but I'm Dawn's stepmother," Gail responded. I remember feeling so stupid. I knew that Gail was Dawn's stepmother. I didn't mean to sound so absentminded, and without going any further into it, I simply shook it off.

"I hope you don't mind my wanting to talk with you," Gail started again.

"No, absolutely not. Just a little surprised, that's all."

Dawn was on both of our minds, yet we didn't speak of her at first. We talked about Derek and the tragedy that was before us. Gail said she had met with Derek's parents and offered to help in any way. We even talked about the mood in the school and how the students were coping with their loss.

"Josh tells me that you were on the bus ride home with Dawn," Gail said.

"Yes, I was," I answered in a shallow but frank voice. I began to tell her about my last moments with Dawn and about the guilt I had carried around with me since her suicide. Gail listened with great interest and curiosity, and when I was finished, she dropped a bombshell.

"You were not the last person to talk to her or to see her, Doug, and even if you were, you are not to blame. None of it was your fault."

"What do you mean? I walked her to the door that day and left," I shot back, knowing that I had done what I said.

"I was in the house that day. I talked to her as well."

Gail went on to explain that Dawn had been dealing with bouts of depression before her suicide and was being treated for that depression. I could see that Gail was trying to assuage my conscience which I'd been battling for 15 years. She, too, had suffered, and for as long. "You're not to blame for what happened to Dawn."

"You're not to blame, either," I stated. Then I told her about the bus ride home and why I refused to attend Dawn's visitation and funeral, as well as my chance meeting at her grave, and that we had made peace with each other, and that I still visit her grave from time to time and leave flowers.

"*You're* the one who's been leaving those?" Gail interrupted.

"Yes, in honor of her memory, not her decision, and because I know that Dawn knows what I know," I said.

"And what's that?" Gail asked.

"That she's sorry and wishes that she could have lived her life, and that she made a mistake. She would take back that one decision of killing herself if she could, but she can't."

I looked at Gail straight in the eye. Both of us began to tear up. That's where we decided to end our conversation. We exchanged numbers and decided to talk again soon.

The next evening, I attended the visitation with our principal, assistant principal, athletic director, and assistant coaches. I was a little nervous meeting with Derek's parents at the funeral home because it is hard to find the right words to say. I was met with an embrace from Derek's father and with a warm greeting from his mother. I expressed my deepest sympathy and offered my services for anything that they needed.

As I was leaving, I was met by former and current baseball players and by Bill Donnelly. Bill stood patiently while he watched parents approach and offer words of encouragement, praise, and support. A few minutes later, Bill approached.

"That has to make you feel good," Bill began.

"It does. I just hope they're right," I answered and looked to the sky.

Bill and I assessed the situation at hand. Our main objectives were to support Derek's family and friends and to prevent copycat suicides that might result from any glorification of Derek's choice to kill himself.

The following morning, we attended the funeral and the graveside service. I met with the baseball team prior to the service, and we drove out to the church as a team. The place was full when we arrived, and we were directed to take our seats near the altar toward the back. Our chairs faced the entire congregation and we had a view of everyone entering the church. There was a muted buzz of whispered conversations as people waited patiently for the family to arrive and the service to begin.

Then suddenly there was complete silence as the doors from the front of the church opened and the pallbearers entered, carrying Derek's coffin. Derek's family walked behind the coffin, which began its long journey down the aisle and to the front of the church. Only the intermittent sounds of someone crying punctuated the stillness. It seemed like eternity from the point that the casket and Derek's family entered the church to the start of the service, and my mind drifted back to the funeral of my friend Kevin.

I immediately felt the old familiar pain. The same sword of sadness was cutting through the room. I also began to grow angry again. I was angry at Derek for creating this pain, this anguish for his family. I was angry at him for bringing confusion and devastation to the team and his friends. I could still remember the pain and hurt that Kevin and Dawn had caused me, and I knew that all of Derek's friends would go through the same pain.

At the conclusion of the church service, I was in the parking lot with most of the baseball team. I was surprised to hear that some of them had decided not to go out to the cemetery. Still others had decided to go, and I accompanied them to the cemetery. As I was driving in what would be best described as the parade route out to the cemetery, I wondered why some of Derek's friends had declined to go. I thought maybe they wanted to avoid the final scene of good-bye, or possibly they were simply exhausted from the ordeal of the last couple of days. Either way, I could certainly understand them not wanting to go out to the cemetery. I went through the same thing when Kevin and Dawn ended their lives. Then I thought that maybe they had grown angry with Derek, as well. I understood, and part of me was hoping that they had grown a little angry.

I began to go into a defensive mode. I knew that history repeats itself, and I did not want a repeat this time. These kids had been through enough. I wanted to be sensitive to their feelings but wanted them to understand that Derek's suicide did nothing to solve his problems. Suicide only creates more problems.

Therefore, the following day, I called a team meeting. I wanted to discuss getting back to business. I allowed the players to speak first. Then I acknowledged how difficult it would be to play without Derek, but we needed to get back to our goals as a team and get back to living. Here is what I said:

"We could just meander through the season and simply take what comes, or we could make our own future and play and live to the best of our abilities. We should do our best, and you know why? Because we're here!

"We're here, and it's good to be here around the people that care for us and love us. And we should not live and play in fear of failure or in fear of not living up to expectations that we set or that anyone else places on us. Simply leave everything on the field of baseball, or life, or anything and everything that we do. And we will do these things because we are here!"

That was my message to the team. We were here and we should make the most of every day and everything that we do. "Whatever is bothering you today will pass, and life will go on. There is more in life to celebrate than to mourn." I hoped my words that day would make a little bit of a difference.

I was naturally worried about copycat suicides and hoped that we had done a good enough job of honoring the memory of Derek and not his decision to end his life.

"Suicide does not make you popular—it makes you dead," I said, ending my speech.

I could not have been prouder of our boys that spring. Both the junior varsity and the varsity baseball teams won their league championships and celebrated their accomplishments together. It was a season and a team that experienced both great tragedy and triumph. At the end-of-the-year banquet, I let the team know just how proud I was of them—not just for winning, but for living and doing the best they could because they were there. We got through the rest of the year without further incident, but it would not be the last time tragedy would strike us.

CHAPTER 9

The Morning Call

The fall of 2005 was a time of great change for me. I had accepted a position as the Permanent Building Substitute Teacher at Bowling Green High School. After Derek's suicide, I wanted to be a part of our students' lives on an everyday basis. As baseball coach, I worked only with the athletes and, even then, it was seasonal. I was looking for an opportunity to work with our students academically as well as athletically, so this teaching position gave me that opportunity.

It had been 16 years since I roamed the halls of B.G. High School, and, of course, many changes had taken place. The entire administration had changed since my years there as a student. Mrs. Carroll had moved away, and half of the teachers had moved on as well. In addition, I had grown from a scrawny 5-foot 3-inch, 100-pound nothing to a 5-foot 11-inch, 185-pound nothing, so the hallways now looked a little smaller than they did 16 years ago.

As baseball coach, I had been in and out of the building many times but had not been in many of the classrooms. Some of those classrooms held many strong memories for me, and while teaching in one of those classrooms early in the school year, I began to struggle with my memories of Dawn. Later that day, I drove out to the cemetery and visited her grave.

I sat a long time in the cemetery that day. I told her of my new teaching position, how difficult it had been, and at least for that one day, I allowed myself to feel sorry for myself and cried. After a while, I got up, kissed Dawn's gravestone, and told her not to worry. I knew she would not want me to feel sorry for myself or live in the past. We had made a deal that I would never do that. It did my soul good, though, to cry and relive some of our dearest memories.

The call came on a weekday. I was awakened by the telephone approximately half an hour before my alarm clock was set to go off.

"Hello," I said, picking up the phone.

"Good morning, Doug, it's Diane." Diane was the high school assistant principal.

"Hey, good morning, Diane. What is going on?" I replied, a little surprised by her call.

"I'm afraid I have some bad news, Doug. We had a student commit suicide last night."

Some time later, it was debated by others whether or not Nick had committed suicide intentionally or not. It was believed by some people that he had possibly died by accident while trying to gain gratification by asphyxiation.

The sound of Diane's voice was understandably shaken, but she was very clear and knew what this news meant to the community and the school. Even though it had been a year and a half since Derek's suicide, the tragedy was still very fresh in our minds.

"You've got to be kidding me!" I exclaimed.

I felt my entire body go numb. Everyone has a phobia that they struggle to conquer. Mine was suicide.

"I wish I were," Diane said somberly.
"Who was it?" I asked.
"Nick."
"I don't know him. I can't think of him," I responded.
"He played hockey and was a member of FFA (Future Farmers of America). He had dark hair," she added, trying unsuccessfully to jog my memory.
"Yeah, okay, I think I've had him in class before," I answered.
"Well, anyway, Doug, we're going to have a faculty meeting at 7:30 in the library to discuss how we're going to handle the day."
"Okay, here we go again," I said instinctively.

I could not believe I said that, I thought to myself, but I knew exactly what we were in for and what lay ahead. After hanging up the phone, I sat at the foot of the bed, rubbing my hands on my face.

"We're never going to learn, are we?" I mused quietly to myself.

My wife, Lisa, had heard only a brief portion of the conversation and then heard my last comment.

"What's wrong?" she asked.
"We had another kid kill himself," I answered.
"Oh, geez, Doug, are you okay?"
"Yeah." And then I got up to start my day.

I arrived at school that morning a little late for the meeting and walked into the library while our principal was briefing the staff on the details that surrounded Nick's suicide. He said that Nick had hanged himself the previous night outside on a tree. Then he read a list of names of people that Nick was close to and asked us to report any behavior that could be interpreted as harmful to themselves and/or to others.

As I was listening to our principal, Mr. Dever, I leaned over to the computer that was sitting on the desk and typed in Nick's name. It was a library computer so I knew that a picture of Nick would pop up. I was still having a hard time picturing him in my mind. Nick's face appeared on the screen, and as soon as it did, I recognized him.

I had had Nick in class before. I remember having a conversation with him one time in the mechanical shop discussing projects that he had been working on. I also remember him as being a nice kid and never being a problem of any kind. What a shame, I thought to myself, shaking my head.

"We have been through this before, folks, so we know what to expect," Mr. Dever commented, wrapping up the meeting. Truer words have never been spoken, I thought to myself.

Students were already bustling about and preparing for school. I was used to seeing the drama that unfolds when a student dies or commits suicide—the locker shrine, the huddling of students, the outpouring of grief, and the rumor mill circulating—but I saw none of this. There was a small team of grief counselors on hand at the school, but I didn't see the usual shock and awe from the masses of students. Nick had many friends, but the mood of the entire school had definitely taken on a different tone.

Nick's suicide did bring some attention, but not nearly as much as past suicides. The experience somewhat paralleled Samantha's attempted suicide. Later in the teachers' lounge, I asked if anybody else had noted the mood in the school. Most agreed with me. One teacher remarked that Nick wasn't a so-called popular kid, worshiped for throwing a pass, shooting a basket, or hitting a home run. I understood that. I had heard he was on the hockey team, and I knew he was involved in FFA, which was the source of most of his friends.

In any given high school, there are different stereotypical groups, and these cliques don't always mix very much or very well. This, I believe, accounted for the difference as it pertained to Nick. It was also possible that some of the kids still had fresh memories of Derek's suicide and were experiencing more anger at the thought of another high school student committing suicide. That surely could have been a part of the reason for the lack of drama.

At the end of the school day, the faculty met again. Many teachers felt the same as I did and mentioned that they, too, failed to see the outpouring of drama from the student body. Another teacher mentioned that we all had gotten better in dealing with the situation, in not encouraging the locker shrine and the early dismissals, etc. The principal agreed but cautioned against becoming complacent. He also reminded us of the group of friends Nick had and that some of them were really struggling with the loss of their friend. He also reminded us to please come and talk with him if we had any concerns about a particular student.

I appreciated his comments. Just because we hadn't seen the same outpouring of drama as we had observed in previous school tragedies didn't mean that we still wouldn't have some at-risk students who might already be depressed and be thinking of suicide.

Nick's funeral was held a few days later. I was again sitting in the teachers' lounge late in the day when Mr. Burkholder, one of Nick's teachers, came in, dressed in a suit and tie. Mr. Burkholder indicated that he had just returned from Nick's funeral.

"How did the service go?" I asked him.

"It went fine. It was very similar to what we experienced a couple years ago, just on a smaller scale," he replied. He went on to describe the service and mentioned his disappointment in not seeing many faculty members at Nick's funeral. That got my attention.

I don't know why it surprised me. I didn't even know how many faculty members attended, but I was upset with myself that I had not gone. I'm sure Mr. Burkholder's comments were not specifically aimed at me, but I understood his point. More staff members should have attended Nick's funeral.

I want to be clear about my thoughts on this matter. I felt I should have gone because I was a part of the staff. I'm not endorsing mass grieving or glamorizing of a suicidal death. However, every life is precious and is as important as any other.

I thought about Nick's suicide in the weeks and months that followed, and I was pleased that we had not had any copycats. I recalled the conversation with Todd the day after Samantha had attempted suicide. I remember his words that day, "I think everybody is just sick of it." The mood in the school after Nick's suicide echoed that sentiment.

I chalked up Nick's suicide as another sad commentary on kids who think that dying at their own hands was some sort of answer to their problem. The more I thought about Nick's suicide, the more I thought of all of life's wonders that Nick will miss out on. Nick would never graduate, never go to college, never have a job, never marry or have children, never buy a house, be a grandpa, or move to Florida at retirement. He would never be able to comfort the ones that he loves the most. Ever.

CHAPTER 10

My Morning Off

One of the things I hate doing is going to the dentist. All of that pain and drilling! Just the thought of going makes me sick. Nevertheless, there are some things in life that you just have to do. I made an early appointment, which required taking the morning off, but it was late January and not too many teachers were absent, for it was shortly after the holidays.

Even though my appointment was scheduled for 10:00, I got up at the regular time because my two kids had to get ready for school and my wife gets up at 6:30, so I treated the day like any other day. The only difference was that instead of being at the high school at 7:30, I went to the gym to get an early workout before the dental appointment.

My plan was to go to the gym, be back home by 9:30, change clothes, go to the dentist, and then go to school for the afternoon. I was able to keep most of that schedule except that I never made it home in time to change, and I never kept my appointment.

While at the gym, I ran into a few people that I knew and let our conversation run a little long. Therefore, I was unable to make it back home to change before going to my dentist appointment. "No problem," I said to myself. I would just go to the appointment and then slide home to change before going to the high school for the afternoon.

After the workout, I was driving to the hospital, where my dentist's office is located, and I had just taken the last turn into the hospital parking lot when my cell phone rang.

"Hello," I said, picking up the phone.

"Hey, Doug, it's Jim."

Jim was a friend whose son was on the baseball team. He immediately gave the reason for calling.

"Doug, Tina just called me and said that our son had text messaged her and said that Jeff Laskey tried to kill himself at school."

I was stunned. Jeff Laskey was a member of the baseball team, and I knew him quite well. He had been on the junior varsity team for the past two years and was to play center field for the varsity team this year. Jeff was a great athlete and had a one-in-a-million personality. He could best be described as someone living life at his own pace and by his own rules. I liked Jeff, but Jeff did not come without his problems. Sometimes his greatest strengths were also his greatest weaknesses. Jeff was the ultimate "fan" at sporting events, so much so that his enthusiasm sometimes crossed the line. He often started verbal wars with fans of opposing teams and had difficulty with authority. On the baseball field, too, he had difficulty controlling his own disappointment and temper. At a district volleyball game played at a neutral site and well attended by both schools participating, Jeff had been asked to leave, and our principal was the authority figure who escorted him out.

The next morning when Mr. Dever, our principal, informed me that he was going to be bringing Jeff down to discipline him for his actions the night before, I asked if I could sit in on the meeting. I wanted to let Jeff know that I was at the game and that I, too, did not approve of his behavior. Furthermore, I believed that with my presence in the meeting, Jeff might show our principal more respect and not make his situation worse.

Jeff came down into the office and sat in the chair across from Mr. Dever. Also in attendance was Mrs. Tache, our assistant principal, who also sat across from Mr. Dever's desk and in between Jeff and me. I sat quietly as Mr. Dever wrote the discipline report in front of Jeff. After he completed the written form, he handed it to Jeff to read.

Jeff made a snide remark, which Mr. Dever corrected him on, and then Mr. Dever asked Jeff to sign the form, indicating that he had read it. Jeff refused, which Mr. Dever duly noted on the report. For the next 5 to 10 minutes, I witnessed Jeff make one mistake after another in dealing with his situation.

I asked Dr. Dever and Mrs. Tache to excuse my interruption, but I wanted to speak to Jeff. I told him that neither Mr. Dever nor Mrs. Tache were his enemy, that I was at the volleyball game, and I believed he was out of line as well, and that he needed to accept whatever punishment handed to him and move forward.

I left the office, believing that Jeff understood what I had told him, and felt that he respected me enough to take my advice. I was wrong. Only a few moments later, Jeff emerged from the office, slammed the door behind him, and stormed out of the main office and into the hallway. I looked at the other people in the main office and began to shake my head. A few moments later, Mr. Dever called him back and "unloaded" on him for his behavior. Seconds after that, Jeff left the office in tears.

Shortly after Jeff had left the office, Mr. Dever summoned other students, mostly Jeff's friends, down to the office to discipline them as well for their behavior at the game the night before as well. One of those students indicated that he was worried about Jeff because he left the school so upset and might have mentioned something about hurting himself.

Without hesitation, Mrs. Tache and Mr. Vannett, our dean of students/athletic director, drove out to Jeff's house to check on him. They also alerted Jeff's mother of the possible problem and asked her if she would come home early from work to be with her son. After they spent approximately half an hour at Jeff's house, his mother came home and Mrs. Tache and Mr. Vannett returned to the school. They both thought that Jeff was much better and was a completely different kid from the one in the office earlier.

I was still upset with Jeff because I had provided him with a way out of the situation and he didn't take it. In fact, he decided to go in the opposite direction. Privately, I told both principals that I would not be comfortable having Jeff on the team if I could not predict how he would handle a bad situation. I had no real intentions of cutting Jeff at that point, but I wanted to have a conversation with Jeff about my concerns.

I have never subscribed to the practice of cutting an athlete just because he had a brush with some trouble. I have always viewed high school sports as an extension of the classroom, and I think that we as coaches and educators should not run away from students who may need us the most. Instead, we should use sports as an opportunity to make a difference in their lives. We may even be able to help turn their lives around.

A meeting between Jeff and me didn't take place until just before Christmas. After a winter baseball-conditioning workout, I asked him to stay after and talk about his behavior back in the fall at the volleyball game. I told him his behavior needed to change, and must change, in order for him to play for the baseball season.

In addition, I asked Jeff if he understood the position that he had placed me in by behaving inappropriately in Mr. Dever's office. I reminded him that teachers, parents, administrators, and even his teammates knew of the risk we took by keeping him on the team. People would question the way I run the program if he were to continue with this type of behavior and if I were to let him stay on the team.

"I never looked at it like that, Coach. What can I do?" Jeff asked.

"Funny you should ask," I replied.

To ease his mind, I told him I had no intentions of releasing him from the team as of that moment, but he needed to make amends with Mr. Dever and Mrs. Tache. We talked about how he was going to take steps to change his attitude and behavior so that he would not get into any further trouble.

"I already apologized to Mr. Dever and Mrs. Tache, but I'll write them a letter. I think if I write my apology in a letter, it might mean more to them and show that I am serious about changing my attitude," Jeff explained.

We also talked about Jeff's twin brother, Jordan, who had experienced medical difficulty through most of his life. In fact, Jordan had recently received a kidney transplant from his mother a year earlier. Jeff said he loved his brother and wished he could be healthier.

We also talked about Derek, life and death, and Jeff agreed that suicide was a bad choice. I spoke of my wife, kids, and friends. I related that to the friends and family that he had and how they depended on him. Jeff agreed and mentioned how he couldn't let them down.

We made a pact that we would talk about anything that was bothering us. A simple "how you doing" was to take on new meaning for us. When I left, Jeff was feeling pretty good about himself and his future. I also felt as if I had helped him. For the next couple of weeks, Jeff attended our winter conditioning workouts and did quite well both in the gym and out of it.

A few weeks later during a baseball-conditioning workout, Jeff approached to ask me a question.

"Hey, Coach, I'm feeling a little light-headed. You mind if I sit down for a while?"

"Of course, are you okay?" I asked.

"Yeah, I think it's from when I injured my neck last fall in a baseball game," he added.

Jeff had been injured while sliding into second base headfirst, colliding with the shortstop's knee. For the next two weeks, he had worn a neck brace.

Jeff sat in the bleachers for the remainder of the conditioning session. At the end of the workout, most of the kids were milling around the gym and going into the locker room to gather their belongings. I saw Jeff sitting in a chair looking a little disheveled, and I asked him if he needed anything. He indicated to me that he had a headache and that was all. I quickly checked the locker room to make sure that everyone had left, and when I returned to the hallway, Jeff was lying on the floor, a friend sitting next to him. I asked him two or three times if he was okay, but got no answer. Finally, he opened his eyes and seemed simply to be confused. Then he began talking to his friend, who was still sitting in the chair next to him.

"What happened, man? I must have passed out," Jeff began saying.

I wasn't sure how much of Jeff's condition was real or part of his drama, but I wasn't going to take any chances. I went to the locker room to summon Neil, our trainer, but he had gone home. I went back toward the front of the gym to where Jeff and his friend were still sitting, and

I asked Jeff to call his mom on his cell phone so that I could talk to her.

After dialing the number, Jeff handed me the phone. I spoke with his mom, Jodi, and described Jeff's condition. We discussed whether Jeff should go to the emergency room. After a few minutes of conversation, Jeff assured us that he was okay and that he would have his friend drive him home.

I stayed at the school but called Jeff's mother to make sure that he got home okay. Jodi reassured me that he not only made it home okay, but that he was resting comfortably. I hung up the phone, confident that Jeff was fine, and hoping that it was just another episode of Jeff being a little overly dramatic.

Knowing that Jeff was a dramatic kid, I was not overly concerned when Jim called to say that Jeff might have tried to commit suicide. To be honest, I didn't believe what Jim was telling me. I figured that Jeff had swallowed some pills or possibly tried to slash his wrists or something. I didn't really think that Jeff was in crisis, other than possibly seeking attention. I also knew that even if I was right, Jeff had a real problem, and I wasn't sure I was qualified to help him.

"You know, Jim, Jeff is borderline between wanting attention and having a real problem, and I'm not sure I'm qualified to really help him," I finally answered Jim.

"So you don't know anymore about it? He was taken to the hospital a while ago," he said.

"No, I wasn't even at the school this morning. I'm on my way into the dentist's office at the hospital. I'll take a look and if I see anything out of the ordinary here, I'll let you know."

Just as I said those words, I came into full view of the emergency room wing.

"Well, there is a police car parked outside the entrance door of the emergency room, but there's probably a police car there most of the time," I continued with Jim on the phone.

"That's true, but call me if you find out anything, would you?" he said.

"Will do," I said, ending the call.

I got out of the car and glanced across the parking lot. "I have a couple of minutes," I thought to myself, checking my watch, so I headed toward the emergency room.

I still didn't believe that anything serious had happened to Jeff or that he was even at the hospital. Rumors fly at the high school and very seldom are any of them true. I treated Jim's son's text message to his mother as just that—a rumor or miscommunication.

I was wrong. As I reached the emergency room doors, I saw one of Jeff's closest friends outside. Louie, as his friends called him, was pacing outside the ER, and he was crying.

"Louie, what's wrong?" I asked.

"I don't know, man," Louie answered.

"What do you mean you don't know? You're out here crying," I insisted.

"It's Jeff. He's in there," Louie responded, still in a daze.

At that point, I knew there was a problem that was bigger than Jeff just wanting attention. Something had definitely happened. I began to believe that Jeff really had tried to kill himself and seriously began to worry.

"Is he okay?" I asked.

"I don't know. They won't tell us anything," Louie repeated over and over.

Just then the doors to the ER opened and Kevin, another friend, emerged.

Kevin was crying uncontrollably. I went closer to him to embrace him and offer some comfort. Before I could reach Kevin, he just looked at me and said over and over,

"He's dead, man! He's dead!"

My body became numb. I hugged Kevin. All I could do was hold him and say how sorry I was that he had to go through this. After about a minute that seemed like an eternity, the doors to the ER opened again. This time it was Jodi, Jeff's mother. She came over to me, and I gave her a long hug as well. Jeff really was gone. I didn't know any of the details or how he died, but I remember Jim telling me that he had attempted suicide.

My mind began fast-forwarding to the next few days, what we all would be going through—again. I then found myself wandering around on the sidewalk with my hands over my head.

"Doug," I heard my name from a voice behind me.

I turned around and saw Bill. As quickly as I turned to face him, I turned away and looked to the sky. I didn't mean any disrespect, but every time I see Bill, I think back to Kevin, Dawn, Derek, Nick, and now Jeff. I put my hands back on my head and began repeating out loud,

"This is a joke. It's a freaking joke!"

I must have said that 10 times. All I could think of was suicide and death. I could see the students at school in pain again, the crying in the hallways, the scene that would again play itself out at the funeral home during visitation and the funeral itself. I could see it all, and that's why I just kept saying over and over again, "This is a joke."

"Can you believe this crap?" I said, turning back toward Bill. He just looked at me. There really was nothing that he could say.

"How did this happen, Bill?" I asked.

"He hanged himself in the bathroom," came the reply matter-of-factly.

"He hanged himself in what bathroom?" I continued asking.

"At the school. I don't know many of the other details," Bill answered.

"Jesus!" I said.

I put my hands back on top of my head and began to wander around the sidewalk again. I knew that I had to get it together. If I was going to be of any help to anyone, I had to put my own personal pain aside and concentrate on others. I grabbed my cell phone and called the school to contact our principal, Mr. Dever.

I informed him that I was at the hospital and asked if there was anything that he would like me to do in any official capacity. At first, he asked why and how I even came to be at the hospital. I explained that I had a dentist appointment and that I just happened to walk into this mess at the hospital. He asked me to take names of every student that I saw at the hospital. He explained that while he was only letting students leave the school in the company of their parents, he could not know for sure how many may have left undetected on their own, and he wanted to be able to notify their parents.

I agreed and hung up the phone. Then I glanced back through the parking lot and saw several students walking toward the emergency room entrance. Quickly, I walked back into the hospital and sought out one of the nurses to alert her that more students would be coming, and unless we wanted a bunch of kids wandering around the emergency room, we needed to find a place where they could go.

Meeting rooms were made available nearby, as well as snacks and beverages for the kids. To their credit, the medical staff did a great job that day to help everyone through a difficult time. In the meeting room, the kids signed in at the front and then proceeded to take their seat in the back of the room. I took my seat in the back of the room at a table next to Jeff's brother, Jordan.

There were approximately 25 students and adults present when a pastor from one of the local churches came in and began to speak to the group. As he was talking, I noticed a nurse enter the room and bend over to speak with Jodi (Jeff and Jordan's mother). Jodi nodded her head and then pointed to the back of the room in the direction of Jordan and me.

The nurse came to Jordan and asked if he wanted to visit with his brother. I wasn't ready for that question. I don't know exactly why, but I wasn't expecting someone to ask Jordan or anybody if they wanted to see Jeff's body.

Jordan at first shook his head back and forth and then said, no.

"It's okay if you want to see him, Jordan. Just let me know and I'll take you back," the nurse stated.

Jordan just sat there for a while and then looked at me. It hit me then that maybe Jordan didn't want to go in by himself.

"You want me to go with you?" I asked him.

He acknowledged that he did. We both got up and went out the side door and down the hall. I was still reeling from Jeff's suicide, and now Jordan and I were about to see his dead body.

As we approached the room that held Jeff's body, Jordan stopped short as if he had second thoughts about going in. I gave him some time to gather his thoughts before entering.

"Jordan, you don't have to do this if you don't want to," I said.

"No, I want to," he replied.

"Why don't you take a couple of minutes by yourself if you would like?" I said, trying to accommodate Jordan in any way he wanted.

With that, Jordan nodded and walked into the room. While he was inside with his brother, I spoke with the nurse about the details of Jeff's suicide. Several minutes had passed since Jordan went into the room, and I began to grow concerned. I excused myself from the conversation I was having with the nurse and went in to check on him. A curtain was pulled around the bed, where I found Jordan standing over his twin brother. He was obviously extremely overwrought and emotional. I can only imagine how difficult this had to be for him.

Jordan and I made it back to the meeting room with his family and friends. More students had arrived, some accompanied by their parents, and they were just learning that Jeff had successfully committed suicide. I continued to take names and do as much as I could to provide information and comfort to those who were just arriving. Later, Mr. Vannett (the dean of students and athletic director) came to the hospital to compare his list of students who had signed out at the high school with my list of people that had come to the hospital. Thankfully, there were no discrepancies.

It was becoming clear that nothing more could be done at the hospital for Jeff or his family. Kim, a parent and friend of Jeff's mother, offered to move the students to her house in an attempt to keep Jeff's friends together and provide some comfort and support. Meanwhile, a hospital official asked Kim and me where the arrangements were to be made. We consulted with Jodi, made the call for her, and scheduled a meeting with the funeral home for 1 o'clock.

I drove to the high school from the hospital to gain a better understanding of what happened earlier that morning. In Mr. Dever's office, I found the superintendent, Mr. Dever, Bill, and some CRC counselors that I didn't know. During that meeting, I learned about the minutes prior to Jeff's suicide. Apparently, earlier that morning before school started, Jeff was in the hallway yelling obscenities when he was confronted by a teacher. After being sent to the office, Jeff met with Mrs. Tache, the assistant principal, about the incident. The two of them had a calm and noncombative meeting and agreed that Jeff would attend a "Saturday school" as disciplinary action for the incident. He left the office, proceeded down the far hallway to the back of the building to a bathroom, and hanged himself with a shoelace from one of his shoes!

Mrs. Tache, I noticed, was absent from the meeting. I knew how she must have felt. Even though her better judgment told her that she was not to blame for Jeff's suicide, for now that would not matter. She would replay the exchange between the two of them over and over again, trying to make sense out of it. "What did I say to Jeff? Did anything I say put him over the edge? Was there anything I could have done differently? Why, why, and why?" Only because I've been there, I knew that eventually she would come to peace with that conversation she had with Jeff, but she would never forget it and she would never stop replaying it in her mind.

At the conclusion of the meeting in the principal's office, I spoke with Bill about the days ahead of us, and again, I was adamant about not glamorizing Jeff's suicide. Bill was, as always, on the same page. I felt as if the two of us could almost read each other's minds. We discussed how to best remember and memorialize Jeff but not to honor or glamorize the choice he made.

Then I went to Kim's house to support our kids and talk with their parents. While there, a parent whose son was a fellow baseball player said that she and her husband worried that Jeff's suicide would be glamorized or that people would put Jeff on a pedestal. I assured her that I would do everything in my power to remember and memorialize but not to glamorize. It was comforting to me that I had parental support.

A short time later, I drove over to Dunn Funeral Home to meet with Jodi, Kim, Geri (another friend of Jodi's), Scott (the minister), Bill, Jodi's mother, and the funeral director, Tim Dunn, to help finalize the arrangements.

I hadn't realized it at the time, but I had come to realize it while sitting in the consultation room that with the exception of one, all of the funerals that we had gone through had been at Dunn Funeral Home.

The visitation would be held a day later and the funeral would be the day after that. Scott (the minister), who was at the hospital and the funeral home, had also hosted the wake service for Derek. I felt comfortable talking with Scott as he was a good listener and cared for the kids. I felt that I was not alone, that I had a "second family" in Scott and Bill. They really understood and were a pillar of strength for all of us.

Later that evening, I attended yet another gathering of parents and students. This time, Jodi, Jeff's mother, was the host. In preparation for his eulogy, Scott directed a group conversation in order to hear some of the "Jeff" stories from all of Jeff's friends. It was done in good taste and was well attended by Jeff's friends and their parents. I have always had mixed emotions about having kids gather in one place to grieve and mourn the death of a friend due to suicide. However, since many parents were in attendance, I didn't have any objection.

I felt that most of the kids understood their role in the grieving process as it pertained to Jeff's suicide. They wanted to remember Jeff fondly, they missed him, they wanted him to know they cared, and they wanted to be together and remember all of the good times they shared together. And there was nothing wrong with that. I just wished they had been spared this pain as it was so unnecessary.

The next day, I arrived at the high school to the same hallway scene that I had witnessed so many times in the past. I was happy to know, however, that the locker memorial that I had come to expect was absent.

"Maybe these kids finally get it, and they aren't going to romanticize the suicide or put Jeff on a pedestal," I thought to myself, and I was proud of them.

I spent most of my day checking on students and sitting in on several meetings with the administration. I still had many questions about the timeline of events and how everything happened. I was in the Mr. Dever's office discussing this when he mentioned that most of the events of yesterday morning were on tape. My whole body became numb with the thought of Jeff's last seconds on video.

"You have Jeff's suicide on tape?" I asked in amazement.

"No, but there is a camera that looks down on that bathroom door," Mr. Dever answered.

Bill was also in the office and both of us were interested in seeing the tape. Mr. Dever walked us over to the monitor, where we could see the exact sequence of events.

The video began at 8:00. Jeff could be seen walking into the bathroom. (This took place immediately after he had left Mrs. Tache's office. It was downright eerie seeing him actually go into the bathroom, knowing what he was about to do.)

At 8:01, Mr. Haselbart walked into the same bathroom, then left 30 seconds later and headed back to class. (Mr. Haselbart, who teaches mentally challenged students, was obviously checking to see if all of his students had left the bathroom. The bathroom itself was fairly small, having exactly one stall, one urinal, and one sink.)

At 8:10, an MC (Mentally Challenged) student entered the bathroom and left at 8:12. This student was in the bathroom with Jeff for 2 minutes. (I have always felt bad for this student because he obviously had seen Jeff but most likely did not understand what he had seen and had not told anyone of what we're sure he saw.)

At 8:18, Mr. Haselbart returned, this time to use the facilities, but exited immediately. Clearly he was upset, for he must have seen Jeff hanging from the bathroom stall. Then a custodian arrived, inspected the bathroom, and used her radio to call an administrator. Within 10 seconds, Mr. Dever, Mr. Vannett, and Mrs. Tache ran down the hall to the bathroom. (Later, I learned that they didn't know why they were summoned, only that they were needed at once and that the custodian was in a panic.)

All three rushed into the bathroom, but Mrs. Tache and Mr. Vannett came out almost immediately. Mrs. Tache had both hands over her face and was very distraught. Mr. Vannett could be seen crossing the hallway toward the library to make the 911 call. Mr. Dever, however, remained in the bathroom to attempt to get Jeff down from the stall support frame. Despite his efforts, he was unable to break the shoelace knot without something sharp. There was no audio on the tape, but Mr. Dever was calling out for someone to bring him a knife.

The video then shows Mr. Dever leaving the bathroom and going into the classroom next to the bathroom in search of a knife. Meanwhile, Mr. Glandorf, a science teacher, ran into the bathroom with a sharp object in his hand. With him was the custodian who made the original call to the office. (The two of them cut Jeff down, and Mr. Glandorf began CPR.) Seconds later, Mr. Dever returned and requested the presence of Mr. Cupp, the health teacher, and probably the most qualified person to perform CPR.

Within minutes, a police officer followed by the EMS could be seen entering the back door of the school and proceeding into the bathroom. About 10 minutes later, they brought Jeff out on a stretcher, then went out the back door and out of the building. Jeff was pronounced dead at the hospital.

The tape was difficult to watch, but it answered some questions that I had about Jeff's suicide. For the rest of the day, our discussions centered on other students who might be at risk of a copycat suicide. The guidance staff at the high school, along with the staff from CRC, compiled a list of those students. It was understandable that the school wanted to do everything it could to prevent another tragedy. It's probably a good strategy for any school.

The visitation was the next night. There were almost as many mourners outside the funeral home as there were inside. Jordan was in the next room with his friends, watching a video of his brother. I just sat, listened, and watched the tape with him. Sometimes it's better not to force a conversation with someone. Besides, I think we all were getting tired of the same question, "How are you doing?" Everyone always says "fine" or "okay," but the truth is that we're not okay. We feel like shit!

The next day was Jeff's funeral. It was a Saturday, and the weather forecast called for rain with a mixture of snow. I know this is going to sound strange, but I was hoping that the weather would prevent a large turnout. I didn't want his funeral to turn into a huge, glamorized, sensationalized event. I worried someone might misinterpret all of the attention, popularity, and tribute as a solution for their own problems. As we all know, that attention fades, your family and friends go on with their lives, and you simply become a "remember-when" story.

My hope for a small turnout was not realized. The weather did nothing to deter anyone from attending. The church was packed. By the time I arrived, there was standing room only. Tim Dunn, the funeral director and good friend of mine, saved a seat for Rob, my assistant coach, and me in the front side pew of the church. We were seated next to Mr. Caumartin, the superintendent of schools, and we all exchanged greetings and pleasantries. I said I wished there weren't so many students in attendance, and I wished the weather had prevented so many from coming. Mr. Caumartin nodded his head in agreement. I'm not sure if he truly agreed or not, but I'm sure he understood my point and shared my concern of copycat suicides.

The service was fairly standard. However, the most compelling part was Scott's eulogy—a most powerful commentary on the **True Lie**. Jeff and others who had chosen the same fate believed the lie of being alone, having no answers, and seeing no way out of their depression and pain.

"Who hasn't thought of suicide?" he asked.

"I have. But I have also accepted the truth, and that is that we're *not* alone. There are people who care about us and what happens to us," he continued.

For the first time in dealing with suicide, I began shaking my head, but this time it was up and down and not side to side. Scott hammered home the message that I could never put into words. Suicide was the ultimate **true lie**.

Suicide was, is, and remains all that is false about dealing with our problems. It's true because those that contemplate suicide have bought into the idea that there is no way out. It's a lie because there are better solutions and there *are* ways out.

At the conclusion of Scott's sermon, I was totally blown away. He was able to say clearly what was so difficult to make sense out of. Before leaving the church, I turned to Mr. Caumartin.

"I take it back. I wish every kid in America could have been here to hear that."

"I agree—powerful stuff," Mr. Caumartin responded with a smile.

Scott had planted the message that Harry, Kevin, Dawn, Samantha, Tyler, Derek, Nick, and Jeff should have heard. The answers that they had searched for were not in a garage, a rope, or a gun, but in trusting our parents, friends, teachers, administrators, counselors, and coaches to help them fight their darkest demons. The act of suicide is never an answer. Suicide is a lie.

Rob (an assistant baseball coach) and I drove out to the cemetery. The weather had turned from rain to snow but did not deter anyone from making the journey to Jeff's final resting place. The end of the burial service came in dramatic fashion. Upon Scott's reciting the last prayer over Jeff's body, Jeff's twin brother, Jordan, slammed down some flowers on the coffin and stormed off to the car.

In the aftermath, some of Jeff's closest friends also suffered. Robby was one such friend and fellow member of the baseball team. One evening, as I was coming into the school from the parking lot, I overheard Robby mumbling,

"This is all bullshit. I can't keep it together, and I was at Jeff's grave today."

"Hey, Robby, what's wrong?" I asked loud enough for only him to hear me.

"Nothing, it's nothing. I can't find my glove, and I was at Jeff's grave today," Robby answered.

I let Robby go inside without anymore discussion. However, after I gave my assistants the practice schedule for the day, I asked Robby to join me in the cafeteria to talk for a little bit. We sat down at a table, and I asked him what was wrong.

"I just am having a rough time dealing with Jeff not wanting to be here. And I forgot my glove, and I don't even know why. I'm just in a fog, and I can't think or concentrate on anything," Robby began.

"Slow down. It's okay. I understand," I said, attempting to calm him down.

I couldn't help being a little nervous discussing suicide with Robby. Memories of my conversation with Dawn and

Jeff came rushing back to me, and I was very apprehensive about having another suicide talk with another student.

I took a couple of minutes to compose myself and to decide just how deep I wanted to get into the discussion. But when I raised my head and looked at Robby's face, I knew I had to share, and really share, my history with him.

"Were you in the gym when I spoke to the team after Derek's suicide?" I asked.

"Yes," Robby nodded his head.

"Well, do you remember when I said that I, too, had lost a couple of close friends to suicide?" I asked.

"I do, but I don't really remember what you meant by all that. You never really explained."

He pulled his arms onto the table and gave me an inquisitive look.

"Okay, Robby, I'm going to share something with you that I have only shared with a few people. You could count on one hand the number of people that I have ever told this to. So let's just keep it between us, okay?" I confided.

Robby agreed, and I began sharing with him what I have shared with you throughout the course of this book—my story of Kevin, Dawn, and Samantha. I told him about the funeral of my friend Kevin at the junior high auditorium, and about my conversation with Dawn on the bus. Surprise was an understatement to describe Robby's reaction.

Further, I told him that Jeff and I had had a conversation about making good choices, and how he was going to turn a new leaf. At that point, Robby dropped his eyes and shook his head.

"I feel like I could have done more to help or save him, man." Robby's eyes remained in his lap as he spoke.

"Robby, do you remember telling Mrs. Tache and Mr. Vannett that Jeff made a comment about hurting himself or something to that effect back in November?"

"Yes."

"Well, because you reported it to Mr. Vannett and Mrs. Tache, they drove out to Jeff's house and sat with him until his mother got home. Did you know that? They told Jeff's mom about the trouble Jeff was in that morning."

"No, I didn't know that," Robby said with surprise in his voice.

"Well, they did, so an argument could be made that you helped save his life that day in November," I explained.

"I never knew that."

Robby looked up at the ceiling for a second and then looked at me. "How did he hang himself, Coach?"

"You don't know?" I asked.

"No, none of us do. I mean, we have heard things, but nothing for sure."

I quickly reviewed in my mind whether or not I was about to cross any line by disclosing detailed, private information, but I then remembered how I felt back when I was dealing with the loss of Kevin and Dawn, so I thought to myself, "Screw it. I'm going to help Robby and tell him."

"He hanged himself with his own shoelaces," I said. Robby's eyes opened wide. He nodded and said,

"Yes, that's one of the things I heard. I just didn't think he could have possibly done that. How did he pull that off?" Robby asked.

"Well, that's really the point, Robby. Jeff had apparently given suicide a lot of thought. Robby, I would like to think that I'm a fairly intelligent guy, and I couldn't pull off a suicide in just 10 minutes with my shoelaces if I hadn't already practiced or knew what I was doing beforehand. He had to have thought about this for a long time. That's why I said you may have saved his life back in November. If you hadn't mentioned to the administrators that Jeff had made those comments, he might have hanged himself at home that day."

"It only took 10 minutes?" Robby ventured.

"You don't know the timeline, do you?" I replied with a question.

"No," Robby responded.

I gave him all the details, the timeline, the efforts to revive Jeff, etc. Robby was a little shocked but also had a look of understanding and satisfaction. I was starting to feel good about myself and about making him feel better. But I felt this way when I got off the bus 17 years ago, and when I left the gym with Jeff. I was determined not to be so naïve this time. I said,

"Robby, I have to tell you that I'm a little worried. I hope you understand, but it's about the story I told you about my friend Dawn. I felt pretty good about how that conversation went when I got off the bus. I felt that I had done a good job talking to her and making her feel better about herself, but we both now know how that turned out. I also felt pretty good about the conversation with Jeff, and now I find myself having a similar conversation with you. Please assure me that you are not in a place where you are contemplating suicide."

"Coach, you don't have to worry about me. I would never dream of doing something like that," Robby said, interrupting.

"I hope not, Robby, because I'd be really pissed."

I continued driving home the point that suicide is a bad decision. Robby interrupted me several times and assured me that suicide was nowhere on his mind. He did everything he could do to convince me he was okay. I finally believed him enough to end the conversation and head back toward the gym.

A few weeks later, I traveled out to the cemetery. While standing in front of Jeff's grave, I looked up from his headstone and scanned the entire cemetery. From that point, I could see the graves of Nick, Dawn, Harry, and the victims of the car accident.

"All of my demons are right here in front of me," I said in a whisper.

Wiping a single tear that had held its ground for a few minutes and then had fallen down the side of my face, I turned and walked back to my car.

Chapter 11

More Alarms

I jumped out of bed like a firefighter hearing the station alarm. I had told myself for weeks to lower the volume of the ringer on the phone. I staggered through the dark and made my way over to the dresser to the phone.

"Hello," I said in a tired and groggy voice.

"Hi, Doug, it's Diane."

It was Diane Tache, our assistant principal. This was déjà vu! The last time Diane called me at that hour was when Nick had killed himself.

"This can't be good," I thought after hearing her voice.

"Yeah? What can I do for you?" I answered.

"It happened again," Diane replied.

"Oh, God! You have to kidding," I blurted out interrupting her.

I suppose it was too much to ask thinking that she might have simply been calling to let me know of a school fog delay or something. However, I knew why she had called, and I felt a lump in my throat immediately. Ignoring the part that she had said "again," I still had hoped that whoever had died had not died by suicide.

"Tell me it's not another suicide," I pleaded.

"I'm sorry, Doug, it was," Diane reluctantly replied.

"Oh, Jesus! Who was it?" I continued.

"Christian," Diane answered.

"Christian?" I repeated.

I am terrible at names. It seems I can only remember people by their faces. I have the hardest time remembering people by their names. In any case, the name sounded familiar, but I could not put a face to it.

"Christian was in our OWE program this year and had come to us late last year from Elmwood High School (a neighboring school district). Did you know him?"

The OWE program (Occupational Work Experience) is an alternative school in a real job setting which gives students the opportunity to prepare for a career after high school.

"I know the name, but not the face," I said, answering her question.

"Well, we are going to have a faculty meeting at 7:30 in the library, okay?"

"I'll be there," I said.

"Are you okay?" she asked.

"I'll be fine."

I started to hang up the phone when I stopped myself.

"Hey, Diane," I said with a panicked tone in my voice trying to get her attention before she had a chance to hang up.

"Yeah, Doug?"

"How did he do it?"

"He hanged himself in the backyard," she said in a solemn voice.

A 5-second pause seemed like at least a minute. I raised my hand to my face and stroked the front of my face to the back of my head.

"Yeah, okay," I finally answered.

"Are you sure you're okay?" Diane asked again.

"Yeah, I'm sure. I'll see you in a little bit," I said finally, and then hung up the phone.

It was again debated that Christian had possibly suffered from the same fate as Nick, by asphyxiation.

I arrived in the library just as Mr. Dever, our school principal, was getting started. He began by briefing everyone with the details of Christian's suicide. Counselors from the Children's Resource Center accompanied him on one side and the superintendent on the other.

As Mr. Dever spoke, I slowly made my way over to the computer behind the librarian's desk to do a student search on Christian. The search would provide a picture, and I wanted to put a face on the name. I nodded as his picture came up. I recognized him from the hallways and from eating lunch in the cafeteria last year. A few other teachers standing next to me nodded as well. I was not the only one familiar with our latest suicide victim.

Standing in the back of the room with my arms folded, I surveyed the room. There was nothing really out of the ordinary. There were no looks of surprise on people's faces. Most of the teachers were sitting at the tables listening to Mr. Dever. Others stood in the back of the room, occasionally whispering to each other. It was different from the meeting we all attended after Derek's suicide 3 years ago. That discussion was new and shocking. Nobody could believe that Derek had killed himself. Suicide was a brand-new experience for some of our teachers, and they had no idea what to expect from our students or community. You certainly did not see anyone staring into space or whispering in the back of the library. Mr. Dever had everyone's attention at that meeting.

The more I learned about Christian, the more concerns I began to have. I feared that the outpouring of grief from the students would be different from suicides of the past. I already knew that Christian was a student in the OWE program, and I knew that OWE students did not share the same popularity as, for example, someone involved in athletics or other organizations. I expected that Christian's friends would be emotional after hearing the news, but I didn't feel that their emotions would be as visible.

The disadvantage that we faced in this situation was that it was almost impossible to identify those who may need help the most. I feared that a false sense of security might be felt in absence of mass public emotions. It should never be assumed that just because we don't see large numbers of students grieving that we are somehow immune to future suicide attempts. I'm not suggesting that we should handle Christian's suicide the same way that my friend Kevin's was or that we should go looking for problems; however, not talking about suicide didn't stop any of the other suicides that we had experienced in the last 3 years.

After the meeting in the library, I walked with Tom, a fellow teacher, down to the main office. It was 10 minutes before the bell and the halls were full of students milling around and preparing for their first class. I kept looking for a group huddled together, crying, but I couldn't find any. So far, the scene in the halls was exactly what I expected.

"I wonder if they know yet," Tom asked.

"They know, Tom. I just think it's easier for them not to talk about it," I replied.

"I think they're tired of it, also," he remarked.

I knew Tom was referring to suicide, and maybe he was right. Maybe they were tired of dealing with death and tired of classmates choosing to die by their own hands. Whatever the reason, it wasn't until a few hours later that I noticed some OWE students, along with others, visibly showing emotion.

Later in the day, I covered a class for Mrs. O. That was what her students called her. Mrs. O was the OWE teacher. She was preparing to travel to Penta County Joint Vocational School (a main base for the OWE program), where many of Christian's other teachers and friends were. Mrs. O was fumbling about, attempting to gather her belongings when I entered her room.

"Slow down, it will be okay," I said walking into the room.

"I just have to get over there," she said in a panic.

I tried to make conversation to slow her down a little. The last thing I wanted was for her to have an accident on her way to Penta. My plan worked for at least the moment. She took a deep breath, looked me in the eye, and softly asked,

"How did you handle this?"

"Unfortunately, with practice," I answered.

I let her know that you never totally recover from losing someone to suicide, but you learn to move forward. Mrs. O shared some of her thoughts, and in our brief conversation, I knew that her head was in the right place. She knew that she had to be strong for her students, and I had no doubt that she would be. I knew what the next few days had in store for her, and I did not envy her one bit.

As for me, I knew exactly whom I had to keep an eye on. I made a point of talking to the friends of Derek and Jeff. I wanted to make sure that they were doing okay and hoped that during those conversations, they would convince me that they were okay. In addition, I wanted them to know that if they wanted to talk, I would be available. For the moment, I wasn't too worried about them; however, it would only be a matter of hours before my concern would intensify.

Two days later, we learned of the suicide attempt of a student who had graduated the previous year. Bob tried to hang himself but had phoned two friends prior to his attempt. The two girls took his threat seriously, went to his house, and were able to get Bob down and to save his life. Bob spent a night in the hospital for his injuries and then spent some time at a psychiatric ward in another hospital for his emotional problems. I asked the same question everyone asks when hearing of a suicide or an attempted suicide. *Why?*

Most clinicians would probably say that Bob really did not want to commit suicide because he called friends first to tell them his intent. I don't know about all of that, but I do know that he had a rope around his neck. That's serious enough for me.

There was no avoiding the issue of suicide the next day at school. Our halls were now filled with even more guidance counselors, and the students could not avoid talking about the latest round of emotional madness. Students speculated about why Bob would want to kill himself. I heard stories of his friendship with Christian as one reason and his recent bout with depression as another. The truth was most likely a combination of both. Regardless of the reason, suicide was back on the front page of conversation at our school. No one, however, could have predicted what was yet to come.

Only 3 days after Christian's suicide, we learned that a third and a fourth student had attempted suicide. The third by taking pills and the fourth by driving his car into a semi. Both miraculously lived through their suicide attempts, but it would be a while before their emotional wounds would heal.

Trying to function at school with any degree of normalcy was pretty much out the window. Teachers walked on eggshells and students looked at each other, wondering if they were going to be the next to attempt suicide. I saw our superintendent at our school building so much that I was beginning to think they had moved his office out there! I sympathized with our administration. Not only did they have to do everything in their power to help our students, but also they had to answer the community, which was asking in a loud voice,

"What is going on at Bowling Green High School?"

No one wanted an answer to that question more than our principal. Mr. Dever's days were filled with conferences with parents, students, counselors from Children's Resource Center, and community leaders. All of the meetings were designed with two goals in mind: to assist students coping with their losses, and to implement some sort of plan to prevent any further suicides or suicide attempts.

A week later, Mr. Dever sat in on what I considered to be his most important and productive meeting of all. In an attempt to hear from the students directly, he scheduled six separate meetings of no more than 30 students per meeting. His idea was simple: give the students a chance to be heard and let them suggest ways to avoid any further tragedies.

In addition to the students, Mr. Dever invited counselors from the Children's Resource Center, any teacher who wanted to attend, and a few private grief counselors from the community. The student turnout was tremendous. The maximum number of students was met in each of the six meetings. In total, half of the students in the school attended one of the meetings. I decided to go to as many of the meetings as I could. I had always felt that listening to our students was the best course of action, and I thought from the very start that these gatherings could be the most productive and the most beneficial. Regrettably, our school didn't offer any sessions like this when my friends committed suicide nearly 20 years previously. Too often in our society, adults only listen to and take advice from the so-called experts and do so without any input from those who suffer directly. These meetings gave our students a chance to be heard.

"Folks, I would stand on my head for the next 10 days if I thought it would stop what's going on here," was one of the first things I heard Mr. Dever say.

I understood his frustration. Mr. Dever was a military man, accustomed to approaching a problem rationally, but there was not a logical answer to this problem, no quick fixes, no magic wand, or secret formula. The best that we can do is to help identify those who are in need and help them in their fight to keep their lives. Moreover, that was exactly what this meeting was all about, to hear from the students in the hope of having them provide us with some information that would help them deal with some of their demons.

The extent to which the students participated in the discussion was impressive. I was amazed at how much they contributed and how they fed off each other's ideas. I was also surprised at how much they offered of themselves. One female student courageously announced that she suffers from depression and frequently finds it hard to cope with the stresses of school. Another revealed that it was very difficult to face his day-to-day routine and to go about his normal activities without his friends who were no longer here. He suggested that it might be easier to deal with a loss if there were a place, a "safe place," as he called it, where students could go and talk without interference from teachers or counselors. However, a third student talked about the anger he feels whenever he thinks about what his friends did to him. He didn't want to talk about it, and he thought that if everyone would simply stop giving it so much attention, it would go away.

My head jerked up when I heard his comments. When I was his age, this was exactly the way I felt about losing my friends to suicide. I was still processing that remark when Robby (the baseball player I talked with after Jeff's suicide) spoke up.

"How do you feel about that, Coach?"

I was caught completely off guard! I sat and stared at Robby for a moment and then scanned the room and noticed all eyes on me. I looked back at Robby, and he nodded his head as if to say, "Go ahead and tell them." I leaned forward and then began.

"I felt angry, also," I contributed.

Again, surveying the room, I saw more confused faces this time.

"Some of you may or may not know, but this is not the first time suicide has plagued our school. When I was your age and a student here, I lost one of my best friends and a former girlfriend. Prior to that, I had also lost a neighbor and almost lost another classmate after she shot herself on the high school track and lived."

Looking around the room, I could see some students shaking their heads, some with mouths gaping, and the rest nodding, as if they knew of the past tragedies. Regardless of their knowledge of the past, I had instant credibility with them. At that moment, I was no longer a teacher, a coach, or an adult acting as if I knew what was best for them. They were looking at me as if I were one of them.

I gave them an abbreviated version of what took place at our high school almost 20 years ago, before any of them were born. We spent the next 20 minutes sharing stories and talking about how we felt about our friends who had decided to commit suicide. It wasn't until the end of the meeting, though, that Mr. Dever asked the million-dollar question:

"So, folks, what is the answer to stopping this kind of activity? What can we do to help our students?"

In all the sessions, that question was followed by silence. Although there were no definitive answers, the common denominator in all of the student groups was that they wanted to be able to talk with someone—but without having the guidance counselors breathing down their necks. They feared that opening up to a counselor would lead to more counselors, which would, in turn, lead to their being labeled as "crazy" by their peers. Others added that they simply wanted to be able to talk with a nonthreatening figure.

"Can't we just talk to someone without having to see a shrink?" was the comment I remember the most.

That response did not come as a surprise to me. It was exactly how I felt 20 years ago. The real difference, and part of the problem in identifying at-risk students, is that our young people tackle the issue from a different angle than do our counselors, administrators, teachers, and adults in general. Our students are scared of suicide. In some cases, the suicide of one of their friends or classmates can be their first experience with death. They internalize questions about their own mortality, life after death, why and how someone could even commit such an act, and what their peers may think of them if they admit to having mental issues and depression.

How can we blame our kids or be shocked when they do not want to talk to us? If you are an adult reading this book, let me ask you a question. When was the last time you had a conversation with your friends about mental illness, depression, or your deepest, darkest feelings? Perhaps we should all lead by example.

Adults, experts, and school officials tackle suicide and mental illness from a completely different angle. They sometimes walk the fence with their response to a school suicide. I genuinely believe that they want to help but are not sure how to do so. They also have to protect their ass. I do not mean to say that with any degree of disrespect, but they do.

Imagine if (as in the case of my school) one student after another committed suicide, or attempted suicide. Many, if not most, in your community would ask, "What on earth is going on at the school? What are they going to do about these suicides before it happens again?" Human nature is great, isn't it? We naturally want to blame someone for a problem instead of looking ourselves in the mirror and being part of a solution.

I believe the people of Bowling Green, Ohio, are lucky. In the face of much criticism, our administrators have done a great job of balancing the issues of the students and the community. I have to believe that there were times they wanted to go home and never come back. I think about the day Jeff hanged himself in the bathroom and what our principals and teachers went through attempting to save his life. There is no manual or class that prepares you for dealing with that.

To answer Mr. Dever's question—"How do we stop our school's suicide problem?"—in my opinion, the answer lies with our society and the perception we hold of mental illness. Depression is a medical condition, no different from cancer, and if gone untreated, can, and will, have the same devastating results. Our society must move past old beliefs and learn to be more open-minded if we are ever to conquer and defeat the demon of depression and suicide. It is true that many answers may indeed lie within prescription medication and other medical advancements; however, we as caring human beings must be more tolerant so that those who need help may feel comfortable enough to seek it.

CHAPTER 12

A Message from Coach Merrill

As a coach, I can relate most of life's lessons to athletics. Some of the same lessons that we teach about teamwork and competition help to prepare you for life. In addition, like most coaches, I am continually looking for new ways to motivate my players to do their very best on and off the field.

I wrote this book in an attempt to motivate not only athletes but anyone who may be suffering from mental illness or depression to fight the demon, to continue their fight, and not to give up. You can win your war. You may lose a few battles, but you can win the war by accepting help from others and by having a good game plan.

Let me be the first to help you and to give you some free advice (free except for the cost of this book). Let us call my advice, "Coach Merrill's playbook for fighting and beating the demon."

Play number ONE: Complete your circle of influence.

My grandfather was the one who first introduced the circle of influence to me. He explained that everyone in my life was a member of the circle—not only my family and friends, but also my doctor, dentist, coach, teachers, superiors, and anyone with whom I associated.

He went on to tell me that when things were not going my way in any one particular area of my life, then I needed to examine who or what the weakest link was and change it. No matter who or what it was, he told me to change it. If someone was holding me back or preventing me from getting what I wanted out of life, then I should replace that person by someone better qualified in that position.

"Run your life as if it's your business. If someone in your circle is not pulling his weight, then fire him," my grandfather told me.

He never said that it would be easy; in fact, he told me that it wouldn't be. It would take courage to replace some people who are in your circle of influence, but it's the right thing to do and sometimes necessary to fix what's broken, which brings us to the next play in our book.

Play number TWO: Courage.

You must have courage to fight your demon. Courage does not always mean being tough and never showing that you have feelings. That's called stupidity.

The *Encarta Dictionary* defines courage as the ability to face danger, difficulty, uncertainty, or pain without being overcome by fear or being deflected from a chosen course of action.

I believe that real courage comes from the heart. It includes possessing the knowledge of what is right and wrong, facing adversity straight on, and having the self-confidence to make the right decision. The challenge in your life comes not when you are dealt a setback or a defeat. Your real challenge in life comes when you are forced to decide how you're going to handle your adversity.

Ask yourself a question. Are you the type of person who wallows in self-pity, makes excuses, and finds someone to blame for your fate in life, or are you the type of person that spits in the face of adversity and gets up off the mat and turns misfortune into opportunity? I believe you are who you decide to be. Look yourself in the mirror. If you don't like what you see, then change it and redefine yourself.

If you know that your fight with the demon is intensifying and is becoming increasingly more difficult to fight by yourself, then have the courage to seek help. That's what tough, intelligent, and strong people do. They realize that a part of their life is weaker than another part and get help. You wouldn't go into a gunfight without a gun, would you? Well, then, tell me why you would wage a war against the demon of mental illness without being armed as well.

Your arsenal against mental illness comes in many forms. Weapons may include but are not limited to counseling, support from family and friends, treatment from your family physician, and prescription medication. You should never be ashamed to seek or accept help from any of these resources, for they are your weaponry and first line of defense.

The bigger the war with the demon, the bigger the gun needed, and do not argue with your doctors and those around you who are trying to help. Remember, they are the ones who are seeing and thinking clearly! If you decide not to accept the advice of professionals and choose a path that dives you deeper and deeper into despair, then you are handing the demon yet another victory.

Play number THREE: Set goals.

Earlier in the book, I mentioned goals and the importance of setting them. For those who suffer from mental illness, setting goals for themselves can seem pointless and can be a task that requires an energy that they do not feel they possess. Goals can seem overwhelming, but I believe that is because people are not always realistic about the goals they set.

For example, if you have a goal of becoming a doctor, you should first set an immediate goal to graduate from high school, then college. Then you should study and do well on the MCAT exam, then graduate from medical school, work in a residency program, and finally work in your own practice as a doctor. In other words, break down your ultimate goal into several smaller ones and achieve them one at a time. Be patient and stay focused on your tasks.

If you suffer from a form of mental illness, my advice is to set even smaller goals for yourself. Get out of bed, have breakfast, and take a walk with the sun on your face while you listen to the sounds of nature around you. Tomorrow you can walk even farther, and before you know it, you will be running.

There will be bumps in the road and times when you will feel like climbing back into bed, and if you do climb into bed, don't beat yourself up about it. Tomorrow will bring another day and another opportunity for you to get out of bed and defeat your demon.

In my opinion, goals are the most important part of a person's life. The sense of accomplishment and self-worth is a powerful combination. You should never be satisfied with what you have done. Stay motivated for what you are going to do next. When you finish one goal, set another and then another. Be the very best at whatever it is that you do.

Play number FOUR: Know thyself.

There is something special about all of us. The greatest thing about us is that we are all different, and it is our differences that make life worth living. We are all capable of contributing something wonderful to society. The difficult part of growing up and maturing is figuring out how and what to contribute.

Too many times in our society we worry and fret about being "normal." We give entirely too much credit to society, and we allow it to define what is normal. We should respect the laws of society, but we should also respect what truly makes us happy, and we should focus on what makes us who we are.

If we choose the alternative and spend our lives trying to conform to what everyone else thinks, we will live short and unfulfilled lives. To our knowledge, we are here only once, and we should grab all that life has to offer.

If you are between the ages of 18 and 24, try not to spend too much time worrying about the next step in life and where you think you should be at this point in time. True happiness does not have a timetable and eventually, you may even surprise yourself with how you want to spend the rest of your life. It's okay to change your mind and the direction of your life.

Play number FIVE: Accept help.

Many times in my life, I have been embarrassed and ashamed of something I have felt or done. In our society, we have been made to believe that mental illness is an issue to fear and hide from, but I refuse to allow society to decide for me what I'm going to fear, and I made the decision long ago not to hide from anything.

Mental illness, taboo in society or not, can be treated and defeated by utilizing a variety of resources. There are psychologists, psychiatrists, medications, support groups, and organizations that are geared to fight this demon. Take advantage of some or all, but use whatever is necessary to win your war against the demon.

The most important part of life is living it to its fullest. This cannot be accomplished if we are not mentally healthy. *Encarta Dictionary* defines mental illness as any psychiatric disorder of the mind that causes untypical behavior. I interpret that to mean a medical problem. I also view a broken bone, cancer, diabetes, or any other physical illness as a medical problem, an untypical behavior.

We do not view it as a weakness or an embarrassment to seek help for any of those disorders, so why should we view mental illness any differently? My message is clear: accept whatever help necessary to become mentally healthy and strong. Be damned what society or anyone else thinks. Do the right thing for yourself. Seek and accept help from available resources!

Play number SIX: Stay physically healthy.

Maintaining one's mental health and physical health are compatible strategies. At any given time in my life that I have been mentally the strongest, I have also been physically the strongest. For some, the idea of becoming healthy automatically implies dieting, running, or lifting weights, all of which seem grueling and time-consuming. Becoming healthy and staying healthy does not have to be an arduous task and should not be attempted at full speed.

Start slow. Take a walk four times a week around your neighborhood or at a park. While at the park, play catch with a baseball, Frisbee, or football. Play tennis, go golfing, or go swimming. Becoming healthy can be a fun and an enjoyable experience, and you will be surprised how your attitude will improve with your increased activity.

In addition, you have to eat right. I have always chuckled whenever I hear about new and groundbreaking ways to lose weight. To me, the math is simple. Burn more calories than you consume. Period.

I'm not being naive. I fully understand the challenge that losing weight presents, and it is clearly more difficult for some than for others. Nevertheless, losing weight and getting healthy should always be one of our top five goals and pursuits.

Try to make a game out of it with yourself. Again, make small and realistic goals for losing weight. Don't set a goal of losing 50 pounds, 100 pounds, or more. Stand on a scale and weigh yourself. Then make a goal of losing 5 pounds, and whatever you do, do *not* put a timetable on it. You will only set yourself up for disappointment and a mental setback. The important thing is that you are working toward a goal, and when you accomplish that goal, you will feel good about yourself and be ready to set another goal. Your self-confidence will increase, and your attitude toward life will improve, also. When we feel good, we think clearly, and when we think clearly, we can accomplish anything.

Play number SEVEN: Volunteer.

All of us who live on this planet have the civic responsibility to volunteer. Volunteering is an essential part of our society's growth, and if our society is to survive, we must find it within ourselves to help those who are less fortunate.

I have heard (and I, myself, have said before) that we cannot help everyone. I believe that to be true. We can only help those who wish to receive help. However, it is our duty to provide an opportunity for all to pursue their goals and dreams. Everyone who is brought into this world deserves an equal chance at peace and happiness.

There are many organizations and associations in constant need of volunteers and assistance. Use your passion and skills in life to find how you can best serve your community. Volunteering does not always mean writing a check or working on some large and time-consuming project, either.

Volunteering can mean working at a soup kitchen or helping prepare for a fund-raiser to benefit a church, a sick friend, or a charitable organization. You can volunteer to be a Big Brother or Big Sister, help build or repair a friend's house or barn, volunteer to coach, or help with Boy/Girl Scouts. The ways one can volunteer are endless.

The generosity and power of volunteering has no bounds, and we see the evidence every day in the news. After some of the world's largest catastrophes, people from all over the world gave what they could to help those who were affected. Tragedies such hurricanes, tsunamis, or earthquakes bring out the best in humankind's generosity. Of course, not everyone is in a position to travel around the world and provide assistance in national and world disasters. However, we don't have to wait for misfortune in our backyard to make a difference in a person's life.

While serving as the head baseball coach at Bowling Green High School, I led a team of volunteers that worked on field renovations at our baseball/softball complex. In 5 years' time, we built a locker room facility for both baseball and softball. The building included two locker rooms, two bathrooms, two coaches' offices, a concession stand, and a garage. In addition, we moved and rebuilt a new 3-foot padded block backstop, a warning track that circles the entire field, a new infield, and new bull pens. Further, a second team was formed for fund-raising. Much of the work was completed by parents of players who had either played, currently play, or will play in the program. Moreover, many who had no direct connection with the baseball program offered their area of expertise and accomplished what was needed to complete the project. To all of you, thanks again!

Even those who could not help physically contributed monetarily. Throughout the 4-year project, we raised over $65,000 by way of hosting baseball tournaments, golf outings, dinners, bowling tournaments, and reverse raffles. Our community took the time and energy to build a facility that we could all be proud of. Our student athletes for decades to come will benefit directly from our hard work, but in the broader sense, we all benefited—everyone who invested their time, money, and labor. It feels good to give efforts to a community project. It promotes a sense of teamwork, community, and self-worth. The benefits to those who receive assistance and those who provide it are endless.

Play number EIGHT: Attitude and perseverance.

A strong positive attitude is the answer for all that you desire from this world. It is the most powerful weapon that you possess. With it, you can defeat the demon and accomplish anything you set your mind to. Without it, the demon survives and your hopes and dreams will remain just that.

Perseverance is what we must possess to continue our fight and to keep our hopes and dreams alive. *Encarta Dictionary* defines perseverance as a steady and continued action or belief, usually over a long period and especially despite difficulties or setbacks.

I have read many books that discuss the power of a positive attitude and perseverance. I underline or highlight the passages that have the most meaning for me, and I go back and read them for inspiration. If you have never read or do not own an inspirational book, get one. Read the passages that interest you and resonate with you the most. It is the first step in adjusting your attitude and starting down the road to a healthier lifestyle.

The outcome of our lives will be determined by the attitude we possessed while here. If our attitudes are toxic, that becomes who we are and how we are remembered. Everything that we do is a result of our attitude. We reek of it! Attitudes have an aura about them, and they affect everyone around us. A strong, positive attitude rubs off on people around us, and those people, in turn, begin to think positively about life.

Earlier I spoke of your circle of influence. Do not under any circumstance allow people with a poor attitude in your circle. They will bring you down and bring everyone else in your circle down. Keep positive attitudes in your life. You will not understand the power of a positive attitude until you have experienced it. You will also find that once you have had a positive attitude and have kept it for at least a week that you will begin to crave it. The power that accompanies a positive attitude is addicting, and you will thirst for more as you continue to live your life.

The power of perseverance is the strength and gift that a positive attitude gives us. I believe perseverance also comes from the heart and defines our character. We must never run from a challenge. We must face our challenges head-on and sometimes do what is hard. When faced with your biggest challenges, you must not ever give up. Whatever happens in your life, whatever the situation, you must possess a positive attitude, perseverance, and courage to face your demon and defeat him.

I believe what a good friend of mine once said, "If you think you've lost, you have. If you think you can, you will."

Play number NINE: Find your happiness and achieve your dreams.

Before you can find your true happiness, you must first discover what your true passion is in life. What is it that separates you from everyone else? What do you enjoy doing the most? If you could be anywhere in the world and could be doing anything you wanted, what would that be? Bottom line, *what do you want?*

It may be a tough question for you to answer, and it should not be taken lightly. However, once you have answered that question, pursue your dream and find your true happiness. Do not think negatively. Under no circumstance should you ever tell yourself that you cannot reach your dreams; likewise, never allow yourself to believe that your dreams are out of reach or not important enough to pursue.

All things are possible with your new attitude, your perseverance, and your courage. Remember, establish small goals that set sail toward what truly makes you happy. Most importantly, do not let anyone else smash your dreams. If you want something, make it happen.

Play number TEN: Power up!

"Power up" is a term that I adopted this year. Originally, I thought it would be a good name for a fitness center or gym. However, while I was thinking of ways to keep a positive attitude and digging deep down within myself for inner strength, the word "power" continued coming into my mind. At times when I felt extremely stressed and felt like collapsing, I began to tell myself to power up.

Power that comes from our soul is what I believe gives me the energy and motivation to continue toward my goals. With that power, I believe that I can accomplish anything. Whenever I power up, I feel invincible and feel like taking on the world. I fear nothing and feel enough strength to fight the demon for the whole world. I feel as if I am a drug of my own, and I believe the whole world needs the prescription.

The concept of power up is not arrogance. It is confidence—confidence to help ourselves as well as others. It allows me to understand who I am and my purpose for this world. I listen to the birds, watch a sunset, and walk on the beach and dream. I enjoy life and look for the positive in everything and everyone.

My final message. I wrote this book for those who struggle in fighting against their demons and for those who feel that they are losing their fight. My book is for teenagers, college students, parents, coaches, teachers, and caring people who wish to make a difference in people's lives. I hope you found it insightful and, above all, inspiring.

My wish is that you will have found strength above all else. Although my friends are dead, I hope that by writing this book, I have given meaning to their lives because they cannot do so for themselves.

It has been said that suicide is a permanent solution to a temporary problem. Ask yourself how you want to be remembered and what your lasting legacy will be for those you leave behind.

Live is worth living. There are, by far, many more things to smile about than to be sad about. Stay with us and see for yourself. If I may, I will leave you with one piece of advice: whenever you get down, feel worthless, or feel hopeless, when you think you have hit the bottom, when you feel you have nothing to lose, do me a favor. Before you cash in your chips, POWER UP!

Web Resources

American Association of Suicidology   www.suicidology.org

The Jason Foundation   www.jasonfoundation.com

American Foundation for Suicide Prevention www.afsp.org

The Ohio Suicide Prevention Foundation   www.ospf.org

Suicide Prevention Advocacy Network   www.spanusa.org

Preventing Suicide Network   www.preventingsuicide.com